MW01027124

Divorcing and Healing from a Narcissist

Emotional and Narcissistic Abuse Recovery. Co-parenting in an Emotionally destructive marriage and Splitting up with a toxic ex

Dr. Theresa J. Covert

Table of Contents

Introduction

A narcissist is a selfish, self- centered, and egotistical person. Whereas characters such as empaths are selfless, always considering the well- being of others and striving towards kindness, service and generosity; narcissists are primarily selfish. Furthermore, they simply do not care and have deeply destructive levels of non- compassion. In other words, a narcissist lacks empathy and compassion in their entirety.

Narcissism is defined by overlooking over people's feelings, enjoying or getting a 'kick' off the suffering of others and a twisted and unhealthy form of excessive self- love. Self- love is beautiful, it is a positive thing. Yet to a narcissist, their idea of self- love is expressed in a very detrimental and self- deceptive way. This also reflects outwards into their personal, work, romantic, sexual and family relationships.

In this book, *Divorcing a Narcissist,* we will go through the many varying elements to being in a relationship or partnership with a narcissist and breaking free from their chains. We explore codependency, the stages of being in a narcissistic marriage; how to manage conflict, understand a narcissist's games and overcome any practical obstacles to health and happiness, and finally how to break free, put up healthy and strong boundaries and live your best life.

Healing is an inevitable part of life. Fortunately for you and with the help of the wisdom and techniques for recovery within these chapters, you will be your confident, happy, whole and best self in no time.

Chapter 1: UNDERSTANDING NARCISSISM

Understanding and Defining
Narcissism

N arcissism is not a positive thing to have to deal with, especially with someone you love and once cherished. Assuming that you are not a narcissist yourself and truly can't comprehend the uncaring, uncompassionate, pain causing and egocentric ways of your narcissistic partner, there is inevitably some healing to be had.

Narcissism is often referred to as *Narcissistic Personality Disorder* (NPD) although it is important to know they are not mutually exclusive. Narcissism is the general characteristics displayed- some of which we have already covered- whereas NPD is the term given to those who have developed the flaws and distortions and embodied them as a personality. It is considered a disease or illness to many. However, like with any disease or illness it is not permanent, and this is something that should be recognized even if lightly. Many people who are married to true narcissists spend years attempting to help their partner, rise them up and support them with patience, kindness and compassion. Any disease is something being at *dis-ease* with itself, narcissism is essentially a lack of harmony and unity of the self within. Your narcissistic lover, therefore, has a fundamental 'split' or distortion in their own energy systems.

To truly understand and define narcissism or NPD it is necessary to look at "the empath personality." The empath personality can be seen as a narcissist's personality polar opposite. Essentially the narcissistic and empathetic nature are two extreme opposites. Why is this important to know you may be wondering? Well, a narcissist is attracted to empaths or people with a highly empathetic nature in words almost indescribable. Empaths are like a drug to the extreme narcissist, there is a magnetic chemistry which pulls an empath into the narcissist's orbit. The same is true for empaths. When a highly empathetic person is not healed, balanced and whole within- with terrible boundaries- they allow narcissistic characters into their personal space.

Understanding "The Empath Personality" to Define Narcissism

Referring back to empaths being polar opposites to narcissists, narcissists become drawn and *magnetized* to the caring, giving and selfless nature of an empath. Narcissists love to take when empaths love to give. Furthermore, empaths are known for their massive hearts, unconditional sense of compassion and natural tendencies to take on roles such as the 'caregiver', 'counsellor' or 'healer.' There is a strong sense of selflessness present within the empathetic personality, they will happily give freely of their time, energy, resources, love, affection, or even money. There is a sense of *beautiful and naive trust* present in empaths or those with highly empathetic natures.

Empathetic Qualities

When discovering the qualities of the empath personality, which you are bound to embodying when finding yourself in a partnership with a narcissist; it is a good reminder to remember your intentions for personal healing and recovery. Just because a narcissist has some unfavorable and highly hurtful beliefs, behaviors and ways, it doesn't mean you have to lower yourself in the name of 'equality'. This is the key to understanding your relationship with a narcissist and the key to getting through a divorce.

"The Empath Nature"/ Empathetic Qualities:-

- Understanding.
- Compassion.
- An ability to connect with others on a deep level.
- The ability to 'read minds,' feel feelings and know exactly what it is like to be in another's shoes.
- Caring and a sense of nurturing.
- A deep love and respect for nature, others and animals.
- Sensitive and considerate to others' needs.
- Usually found in some caring, creative, healing or service- oriented field. Many empaths or highly empathetic people work in charity, care or support work, counselling, spirituality fields or mediumship, humanitarian projects, animal welfare, or as a nurse, physician, healer, therapist; or any other service profession relating to helping others.
- Advanced and higher frequency emotional functioning.
- Aware and conscientious.

- Conscious of their surroundings, environments and personal relationships.
- Creative, artistic or uniquely gifted. They use their artistic and imaginative gifts and abilities to shine light in some way, acting as a channel for higher thought forms, idealistic and compassionate concepts, or 'genius' perspectives that will benefit others.

Being aware of this can aid in your understanding of narcissism and all its many implications as a narcissist gets drawn to these beautiful and positive qualities and seeks to destroy them, further causing pain, suffering and chaos on their path.

Now, if we look to the *characteristics of a narcissist* you will see just how polar opposite and dualistic empaths and narcissists are.

- Selfish.
- Self- centered.
- Egotistical.
- Vain.
- Insensitive.
- Lacking any if not all empathy and compassion.

- All about 'number 1.'
- An unhealthy sense of entitlement.
- Deceptive.
- Manipulative.
- 'Feeds' off the pain and suffering of those they claim to love.
- Unnurturing.
- Unresponsive to others' feelings.
- Extreme and exaggerated feelings of self- importance.
- Unhealthy self- esteem and self- wealth.
- Self- delusions and inner traumas masking as confidence and 'empowerment.'

In short, a narcissist causes pain and suffering to those they love and the unfortunate truth is they don't care. It's all about 'number 1' and narcissists are some of the most selfish and addictive personalities you will ever meet. *Karmic entanglement* is also often present. Karmic entanglement, or karmic exchange, refers to entering into unhealthy or destructive exchanges, ones where the narcissist gives out harmful or hurtful energy and thus becomes a part of a cycle. This cycles becomes recurrent and repetitive until they can learn to transcend their karma, look at the lessons inherent, and evolve from them.

For a narcissist, this can be very difficult as it involves considerable levels of compassion, self- forgiveness and empathy; which is virtually impossible for someone with NPD. For you this means that you unconsciously and often unwillingly enter into these karmic entrapments. Notice the use of the word 'entrapment.'Karmic exchanges are usually exchanges, a mutual agreement by two individuals to learn from one another, evolve and grow together and individually. Yet, with a narcissist karma is an entrapment, quite simply because what you expected to receive and experience is the literal opposite of what you get. A 'normal,' caring, kind and warm- hearted person has no clue as to the true nature of a narcissist and therefore couldn't possibly comprehend that the relationship would turn out the way it does. Remember, narcissism is often called *Narcissistic Personality Disorder*.

So, because you don't consciously choose to become involved in such a destructive, uncaring and hurtful relationship, at least not at face value, your connection can be seen as an entrapment. Karma in its independent expression is not necessarily negative, it can be a beautiful exchange of energy; full of self- discovery, growth, personal development and self- evolution. It is only the narcissist's ways which make your entanglement an entrapment.

This is one of the main topics we will explore in later chapters. Feelings of shame, issues of self- worth and self-esteem, and a general 'underlying depression' can all be a result of being with a narcissist for a long period of time. However, the key to your recovery and healing is to recognize that *you are not your partner*. We are all individuals and your beliefs, perspectives, attitudes and actions are not representative of your narcissistic partner. Once you understand this full and integrate the teaching, you can finally be free. Personal freedom is highly attainable.

"The Codependent - Narcissist Dance": The Perfect Dysfunctional Relationship

Unless you are completely autonomous, self- sovereign and independent you are most likely codependent in some way. This is because we are all *co*- dependent, to an extent. We all have innate capabilities and capacity for community, co- operation and co- existence, and with these come a natural level of codependency. In normal (aka- non- narcissistic relationships) this isn't a massive problem and can actually lead to some beautiful connections and healthy attachments. However, this innate tendency towards codependency can be a major problem when dealing with a narcissistic friend, lover or partner.

'The Codependent- Narcissist Dance' is therefore referring to the *natural* and *innate* tendencies any and all human beings have towards their partners when in a relationship. This does not mean that you are codependent or have personal problems with codependency, it is only referring to the energy exchanges and interaction between yourself and your narcissistic 'other' (partner, husband, wife, or lover).

Unlike in normal relationships and marriages which are loving, affectionate, kind and warm- hearted, mutually respecting and supportive, and also with deep and sufficient levels of intimacy and inspiration (lifting your partner up when they need it); a connection with a narcissist is nothing like this. They are inherently selfish with a primary disregard of your feelings. 'Compassion,' 'empathy' and 'sensitivity to your needs' do not play an integral part to their reality.

The best way to understand what occurs in the 'dance,' on a deeper level, between a loving and normal- oriented relationship and one with a narcissist, is to look at the differences between the intentions, motivations and energetic exchanges present. The table below covers quite a lot of significant points to further develop our discovery.

'Normal' Relationship	Relationship with a Narcissist
Affection, raw or vulnerable emotion, deep and sincere feelings, authenticity and honesty.	Manipulation, emotional deception, gaslighting, white or severe lies, arrogance, pride and egocentricity (on the narcissist's behalf).
An emotional desire to be close intimately, romantically and sexually.	The emotional desires of exerting their will and making you feel small or down. Wanting you to be powerless, jealous, confused, intimidated, vulnerable, fearful, angry or frustrated.
Mutual feelings of trust and respect.	Little to no real respect (there may be an illusion sense of respect present when in social settings).
Thinking and feeling in terms of a partnership; values such as cooperation, communication, empathy, consideration, harmony and 'we' are present.	'Me,' 'mine' and 'I' often replace 'we' and 'us.' There is little to no consideration of actually being in a *partner*ship.
A sense of inspiration- both partner's inspire one another to be the best versions of themselves; or at least support one another.	A genuine lack of care for their partner's (your) self-development, happiness, success or personal goals and dreams coming true. It is all about them.

Specific Focus: Elements of this Dysfunctional Relationship

In a dysfunctional relationship you and your partner 'bounce' off each other. Daily interactions, real energy exchanges; these are defined by an unwanted and unwilling entered sense of codependency which comes with the codependent- narcissist dance. It can be an extremely unconscious act entering into a relationship with a narcissist. At first they appear charming, friendly, 'nice' and kind- hearted; there is a real charm to them. However, over time this charm become diluted and their real colors begin to show. Once you are in a relationship with a narcissist it can be very difficult to recognize that there is a strong element of codependency involved. This is because they have literally magnetized you in- you are entwined on a deeper level than meets the eye. This is why we refer to the interactions present as a *dance*. You and your partner are energetically entangled.

This would be OK and even amazing if they weren't narcissistic, but the sad truth is that the agreement you have unconsciously entered into is full of pain, confusion, suffering and endless self- doubt. Regardless of how strong, centered and self- empowered you are, a narcissist can always make one feel unworthy in some way, or question yourself to the points of low self- esteem and near complete destruction of self- confidence.

There are many different angles when exploring your relationship so the best way to do this thoroughly is to break it down into stages.

When talking about work

When you are talking about work there is a strong element of *dismissal*. A narcissist neither supports you fully nor do they truly care. Your successes, achievements, victories and soulful passions are of little importance to them. What would be provided in a normal partner's happiness through hearing of your happiness, there is instead a cold indifference. If you are dealing with an extreme narcissist then we could even go so far to say that they get annoyed, irritated or upset by your successes. There is virtually no support or joy for you. It is in these situations when a narcissist's true selfish ways shine through. Furthermore, they don't care about hiding their true feelings or even pretending. It is almost like they want you to know that they have little to no positive feelings towards you, and they are happy for their ego to be seen in all of its (false) glory.

The key to remember at this stage is that narcissists thrive off people knowing who they are and still choosing to bend to their will, or play their games. What may be deeply disturbing, embarrassing or intolerable to a normal person is perfectly acceptable and encouraged to a narcissist. Many behaviors and actions which makes us feel awkward or extremely compassionate actually *feed* the narcissist's personality. Quite simply, they get sparked from others' reactions.

Yet because their personality and the identity they have created are so strong, they get away with it. People still remain in their orbit (for the most part), family still love them and friends and romantic partner's still cling on to the initial charm and brilliance they once knew and loved. Narcissists can be very, very clever! Relating to work, this means that when you are in a balanced, grounded and mature space it is harder to accept or even contemplate that you have chosen a partner who is so not on your wavelength.

"How could I possibly let someone so indifferent and selfish into my personal space?"

"I thought we were on the same wave, where did I go wrong?"

"I truly believed s/he was mature, wise, brilliant and beautiful. What on earth is going on?"

These are just some of the questions you may find yourself asking. Forward thinking, luckily you can recognize these signs and learn to shape your own path. There will always come a time when you realize just how selfish and cold your partner, and supposed lover, can be. When this moment comes (or when the final moment comes and you are finally ready to leave the cycle) the epiphany that your career, heartfelt goals and dreams, and personal aspirations are far more important than any tolerance of disrespect, abuse and neglect. *You are worthy* of having a partner who supports and listens to you, cherishing your work and passion in all you do in the process.

When with friends or family

Being around family with a narcissistic partner can be very tricky and also painful. Why? The answer is very simple. When you are at home or alone you are the target or their abuse. You are either a direct victim or if you choose a path of attempting to rise above victim, you are certainly the sufferer in the relationship. You have to go through endless attempts of lifting your partner up, helping them see the light and putting the energy into showing them a better way. You find yourself exhibiting vast levels of compassion, patience, kindness and empathy, which all take a lot of energy from you. Simply put- it can be very disheartening being with a true narcissist.

Yet, when you are around friends and family nothing is wrong! They are the life and soul of the gathering, and furthermore they are still charming and lovable. This is the persona a narcissist wants to display, they want to appear in a beautiful, shiny and positive light. Because of the strength of both their character and illusion, it can be virtually impossible if not self- harming to try and break this illusion. Any words, opinions, actions and attitudes displayed in front of others which even verge on showing the narcissist in their true light can cause a seemingly never- ending cycle; a cycle which even the strongest person cannot deal with. Your partner may turn on you, or they may twist things so severely that the only thing you can do is to "shut up,' stop talking or appease them. They will suppress you and silently bully you into conforming.

It is not necessarily abusive like you see in abusive relationships. The interaction in a codependent- narcissistic relationship is more subtle, the type of 'abuse' being referred to here is their deep and extreme manipulation, deception and emotional trauma caused through their ways. Regardless of your definition of abuse, however, it is still completely disheartening and draining. So, when you are around family your narcissist wife or husband is the perfect partner. They can do no wrong for they are witty, smart, likeable, intelligent, helpful and kind. This kindness and warmth often displayed is of course only a mask and only every shown when around family; they need people to believe them. If everyone was a target of their narcissistic abuse, there wouldn't be anyone to cover for them in times of social need. As we explore in the next section narcissists thrive off social support. It is their key to success.

There will always be someone in your family who you are closest to. Although it may initially be hard to take in and further deeply disturbing and heartbreaking, your partner chooses this person to sweeten. Life is a game to a narcissist and therefore your relationship is also a game. If you can confide in your sister, aunt or father, your narcissist partner will pay extra attention to your sister, aunt or father. Charm, humor, effort, warmth and attention will all be applied to make sure that your ally is their ally. Again, narcissists need someone to help keep their delusions strong, so if the person or people you choose to confide in no longer believe you or see the situation for what it truly is; then your energy and support diminishes. There is a strong aspect of 'energy vampire' in play here, yet the difference is that narcissists get away with it due to their added charm and strong personal vibration.

The best thing you can do in a situation like this is to sit down with the person you feel you wish to confide in. You need to make sure that they know you are being serious and are in need of a real heart to heart. Anything less than complete depth, honesty, vulnerability and self- acceptance of the situation will not do. If there is any form of 'light- hearted' bitching, slander or negative speak this will simply feed the narcissist's game. This is the only vibe they know. So, to truly make your situation known and gain the support you need, make sure you are first serious with yourself before opening up to someone. Taking the right steps towards healing and inevitable break up (if you choose this path) come into this.

When in social settings

Social settings feed the illusions and intended stories of a narcissist. There is an element of 'lone wolf gone wrong' with narcissists, or a lone wolf immersed in darkness and the shadow self! Narcissists need to be liked, yet they are still highly independent in a social group. They make sure to always maintain their own self- worth and autonomy even when they appear to have many friends or admirers around them. This is the trick, they appear to have many friends. In truth a narcissist doesn't really have any friends as they are selfish and manipulative, also being all about what they can take and how they can deceive. Thus, to an outside perspective they are sociable, charming, extroverted and friendly with a good heart and a healthy mind; although internally there is another story. The hidden intentions and motivations of a narcissist are to use and manipulate people to ultimately benefit their own self

24

in some way, and it is important to have at least a couple of people on 'their side' who they have a strong hold over.

When the time comes everyone is expendable to the narcissist. Even you. This is the hurtful part and the reason why it can take so long to recover from a narcissistic relationship or marriage. You have been their rock, their gem, their support system and their subtle yet guiding light. Presuming you are not a narcissist yourself, you have spent months to years being patient, kind, compassionate and caring, also doing your best to have a healthy, loving and harmonious relationship. You have had to put up with appeasing your partner when with friends and family, or being suppressed to keep their personality manipulations in tact. Simply put, you have already suffered a lot.

So when it comes to those few groundbreaking moments in social scenarios where you really and truly need a partner, a soul mate and a best friend; this can be your key moment. Once or twice is an in the moment action, a couple more times is a habit or repeated behavior, but permanently and perpetually is a cycle. You do not want to get entwined in the cyclic treatment from a narcissist!

When alone

When you alone together this is where the true signs of a dysfunctional relationship come out into the limelight. It is virtually impossible if not impossible for a narcissist to hide their true colors when alone with you, one- to- one. You are trapped in an endless cycle of giving and taking, yet this giving and taking is not balanced nor is it just. Let's look at the characteristics of the giving- taking cycles present in this relationship.

- You recognize something is not right and start to see the 'narcissistic shadow.' Because you want the relationship to work, and because you truly love them, you begin a route of compassion, patience, active assistance- trying to help and steer things in better directions; empathy, mindful and intended communication, insightfulness and enhanced energy. Your enhanced energy means that you always go that extra mile to try and reason with your partner and make them see sense. You may also sporadically do moments of the opposite- attempting to 'match their vibe' and resort to brief frustration, anger, impatience, intolerance or upset. In a normal relationship these tactics may work as you realize everyone is capable of compassion, further admitting when they are wrong and returning to the light. Yet in this relationship all of your efforts and intentions go to waste. There is no reasoning with your partner.

- You constantly feel like you have to dim your light for your partner. You simply are not allowed to shine, be successful, achieve anything above and beyond your relationship, or actively show and experience personal joy and satisfaction in any way. Each time you do you are met with narcissism. Your partner's ego suppresses you and all of your magnificence. This has considerable negative effects on your morale, self- esteem, confidence and a sense of empowerment. Your work, personal or family relationships may suffer as a result.

- If you are already committed to some self- love, self- care or healing practice the only times you feel truly content and free to be yourself is when you have distanced yourself and are doing your own thing. Going for a walk in nature, immersing yourself in some project or hobby outside of your home, and taking sufficient time to be with friends or family helps greatly; however the underlying problem still remains. Being in a relationship with a narcissist can drain you, and even when you have done everything in your power to rise above or take the space necessary to re- charge, your partner does not wish to learn or change. If you are on a journey of self- love and healing then your partner's behavior and overall energy will feel very alien and distorted to you. You will most likely attempt to nip it in the bud as soon as you see the situation for what it is. Otherwise, depending on your choice (instantly leaving or choosing to stay) you will suffer internal chaos and re-sistance through being pulled in different directions.

- The attention is always on them. Their selfish, egotistical, self- righteous, self- absorbed, mean and hurtful, non- empathetic and uncompassion-ate ways are in full effect when you are alone. This is because you are their main target, the main person they feel they can be themselves around. It doesn't matter how terrible, selfish and unkind they are as you still love them regardless. There is a huge element of 'game playing' present, you are seen as easily manipulatable or even gullible and naive. Unfortunately, your narcissistic partner plays off this reality and self- created story. If you allow this game to perpetuate, it can be very hard to break free from as you will have given away your power.

- Finally, the ultimate 'giving- receiving' cycle is in full force and manifests in a number of different ways. Absolutely anything you do, say or believe is met with a complete resistance. You say white so they say black. You shine light, so they express shadow. Compromise, balance, harmony, cooperation and fairness in your relationship are virtually non present and furthermore you are manipulated to feel that you are always wrong, or stupid. Holistically speaking, your partner treats you in a very 'low vibed' and uncaring way.

In the bedroom

Sexually, romantically, and intimately- being with a narcissist is not something one would willingly enter before creating a deep bond. The 'codependent- narcissist dance' is amplified in the bedroom, and at times it is like you are their personal plaything. Take your awareness back to when you first met. They were charming, wise, funny, likeable, lovable, attentive to your needs, sexy and highly attractive. *This is the persona they exhibit to get their needs met.*

Exhibit is not even the accurate term to use; force, push, attempt so hard to portray, trick, manipulate, and execute with utmost intensity would all be more accurate. In short, you are magnetized to their manipulations still holding onto the memories of how things used to be. To further exacerbate this is the fact that you know your partner is (or was) capable of love, real devotion and intimate connection. The thought of them using you, not caring or treating you like their toy for their selfish ends is not something which one would want to even consider, let alone accept as how things are. It is not even just about sex or physical satisfaction. The games of a narcissist in the bedroom are more psychological, mental and emotional. They know that desire, bond, love, intimacy and emotional, mental and psychological merging are natural and healthy, so they play on this. They receive great pleasure from your silent suffering.

This is the ultimate codependent- narcissist dance and once you are entwined in their hidden motivations it can be difficult to free yourself. You may become addicted to the feeling if you are naturally submissively inclined, or you could still be holding onto the hope and belief that this is just a phase; that your partner's true self will shine once more. Heartbreakingly, it won't. This is the true nature of a narcissist.

When you are empowered, or aligned to your own path- purpose- passions

Like with work topics, when you are self- empowered and in a generally 'brilliant and beautiful' space you are like catnip to a cat. Without going into too much detail, your passion, sense of purpose, inner fire and zest or spark for life is too much for the narcissistic personality. It is like dangling a treat in front of a dog, or having a bottle of cold, crystal clear water in front of someone who has been on a five hour hike in the heat. You are essentially a flame waiting to be put out.

This may seem like an excessive amount of analogies, but hopefully they show the extent of the dynamic when you are in your prime! The only thing which is in your control is your response. Will you allow your narcissistic partner to pull you out of your flow and into a dysfunctional and harmful reality? Or will you stand your ground, release

31

this unhealthy codependency and stay fully committed to your truth and self? *Boundaries* are the key here, as is self- love and self- respect.

When you are down or sensitive

Codependency's ultimate manifestation is when you are down or sensitive. It is natural to have moments of weakness, low morale or extreme sensitivity; we all go through cycles and stages. With a kind, caring, and non- narcissistic partner these moments allow your other half to shine, step into their compassion and be a beautiful partner. The elements of support, companionship and being someone's rock are allowed to come forth in all of their beauty.

More generally speaking if you usually suffer from low moods or sensitivity you are the ideal person to be with for a narcissist. A narcissist needs someone to attach to and they equally like to be clung on to. This ultimately expands their power, as your codependence to their narcissism perpetuates and further increases their narcissism. Remember that a narcissist feels genuine joy, peace and pleasure from their ways- they are not seen as an illness or something negative to them.

"Narcissists and Normals":
Why You Are the Perfect Match for a Narcissist

Here are five major reasons why you are the perfect match for a narcissist.

1. Magnetism

There is always some magnetic quality which draws you together, whether that be their *charm*, shared interests or simply your empathy. There is truth in the saying 'opposites attract' and a narcissist is, fundamentally, the polar opposite of non- narcissists (due to their complete lack of empathy, sincere emotion and inner moral compass).

2. Feeding their Personality

You feed them. You feed their ego, you feed their narcissism and you feed their motivations for wanting to inflict pain, suffering or sadness on another. Of course, you aren't responsible for their behaviors or feelings- it is your natural self that feeds their narcissistic personality. Any positive or lovely quality you possess is fuel to their out of control- burning and destructive fire.

3. The Need to Thrive off Others
(to keep their illusions in play)

Illusion is a word strongly associated with narcissism and something in which you unconsciously play to. *Delusion* is also accurate. A delusion is essentially an idiosyncratic belief, recurring thought or impression which contradicts reality- rooted in some sort of mental imbalance or faulty perception. A narcissist needs this not only to thrive but to survive. Their whole reality is dependent on it and furthermore they need others to keep their delusions intact. They achieve this through the fear, intimidation and hurt they cause to others, and the subsequent codependent-narcissist dance their targets become entangled in.

Ultimately your purity of thought, faith and hope or trust that there is beauty, goodness and truth inside of them perpetuates their 'thriving,' and thus makes your true nature the perfect match to their manipulations and hidden motivations.

4. *Deception and Manipulation*

Narcissists are so deceptive and manipulative that they bounce off your honesty and authenticity. They also grow stronger and more powerful in their convictions and illusions because of them. Your characteristics are like sparks to their deceptive and manipulative qualities, making you the perfect match because you have already been enticed by their charm. Remember, the initial narcissist charm and their extreme narcissistic personality traits are part of the same package; they are both two elements to the narcissistic persona and character they have created. In this respect, once you are enticed and under some belief or impression that they are genuine and warm- hearted-nice people, capable of love, intimacy, friendship and companionship; it is very easy from this point to keep you trapped in their game.

5. *Empathy and Compassion*

It has been said before but it needs to be said again. Any person capable of real and deep levels of empathy and compassion are perfect for the narcissist. Unfortunately, this means you and every single person on planet earth who isn't overcome with narcissistic personality disorder or traits have the potential to be entwined in a narcissistically abusive relationship. The words 'magnetism' and 'fuelling their fire' have been shared quite a few times now, but this is because these are the two most accurate expressions to portray and truly understand what is occurring . It can be hard to believe humane, decent and rawly vulnerable and sincere qualities like empathy and compassion are catalysts for pain infliction, joy and happiness from causing suffering to others, and emotional manipulation and intimidation; but it is a reality that, once accepted, can lead to great healing, release and recovery.

Dating a Narcissist

Dating a narcissist is interesting. Assuming that you are already married to one and are seeking divorce, or have already separated or begun the procedures, you will already be aware of quite a few of the aspects involved in the dating stages. If not, however, or simply if you are reading this to seek clarity and look back at your past for self- discovery, healing and release; there are certain signs and red flags to look out for in the dating cycles. It is also very useful to explore why narcissists are so appealing and what they themselves get attracted to.

'The Signs'

The major sign which is the root and stem to all other signs, red flags and things to watch out for is known as the "social factor," or more specifically- "***the social illusion.***" This is, in essence, the charm and social grace or wisdom narcissists show when in social settings. Family gatherings, peer settings, group work, social scenarios with colleagues or peers, and friendship groups or social situations are all prime moments where you can truly see a narcissist as a narcissist, if you are able to play the role of observer. In society nowadays we are predominantly extrovert. It is not normal for someone to be intrinsically and wholly connected to a social group and be sat in solitude, introspection, observation or with a pen and paper, or pencils and drawing pad in hand. These are the type of displays and behaviors which define an extrovert's opposite: introversion. Introverts or those predominantly introspective inclined are highly observant. They do not need to talk much and can be an active member of any group, friendship circle or social setting through their silence and subconscious. Introverts are said to be very much rooted in the abstract.

How does this relate to narcissism and noticing the signs that you may be dealing with a narcissist? Well, for starters you can learn from them and seek to embody their traits. It is very easy to be caught up and seduced into the narcissist's charm, especially when there is always constant noise, interaction and sensory stimuli to keep you under their spell. Yet detaching or withdrawing slightly and taking on the role of the silent yet highly aware observer, just like an introvert or introspective person does, will allow you to pick up on all the clues; and then some! We have both an intuitive and an analytical and logical-rational mind. Many artists, writers, painters, poets, creatives and philosophers or deep thinkers are very much connected to their right brain. The right brain or right hemisphere is related to spatial awareness, creativity, intuition, imagination and holistic thinking and perception. For this reason, it shines through when you become less extroverted and 'go within,' paying attention to subtle senses, hidden impressions and motivations and levels of higher thinking.

And this is exactly what a narcissist fails to see! The thing you need to know about narcissism is that those who have it deeply ingrained as part of their personality are so entwined in their own stories and self- delusions that it is virtually impossible to notice anything but their own world. Narcissists create a reality where they are the center stage, and no one could possibly find them out or expose them because they are so arrogantly and ignorantly confident (even though this 'confidence' is false and not rooted in a real sense of self- empowerment). Thus, in a social setting- if anyone were to be a silent observer, happy and content in their own introspective or highly observant and "of the radar" inner world; a narcissist would be ignorant to it. It can almost be seen as their *blind spot*.

So, to truly see the signs when dating a narcissist, take some moments to step back and play the introspective, quiet and anti- social one of the group. You may even appear as shy, reserved or down- but this is OK. This allows you the space to shine in your own silent way and get to the core of your potential partner's personality. All of the red flags below and knowledge insights in the rest of this book will help you know exactly what to be mindful of. Perhaps even take a journal, notepad and pencil or some artistic and creative outlet with you. No one will judge or even notice as, the truth is, everyone has an artistic side. Be the observer and watch your dating partner's body language, impressions, responses, behaviors and facial expressions intently (yet subtly). You will start to unravel the truth in no time.

Why they are So Appealing

Narcissists have a charismatic charm to them. This charm may only diminish and be replaced with the characteristics of a narcissist's true personality once you have become entangled in the relationship, or are already married. There are some 'blind spots' which add to why they are so appealing. These blind spots are sexual attraction, an innate desire for codependency, seduction, idealization, familiarity and the need for companionship.

1. *Sexual attraction*: It is easy to ignore red flags and overlook your dating partner's narcissistic characteristics when there is such a strong sexual attraction. The main reason why narcissists are so attractive is because of their charm. They are *incredibly* charming, and this makes them even more appealing. Because of the innate human desire for companionship too, the sexual appeal is amplified. The underlying key point with sexual attraction is that, unfortunately, we as a species carry a lot of deep and buried trauma. There is an ancestral quality to this trauma which is often referred to as 'ancestral wounds.' Essentially, we carry thousands of years worth of trauma that is shared and part of the collective conscious energy field. It is part of our psyches and stored in our cells. Reality as we know it can be seen as a sort of dream, however it is a shared dream and there are many characteristics and lessons all humans go through. Karmic and ancestral wounds, trauma and unresolved wounds all stem deep, and it is usually not until adulthood- or if someone begins a profound journey of personal healing- that these deep wounds start to come to the surface. In terms of sexual attraction to a narcissist, this implies

that there is a strong element of being attracted to the pain, suffering and trauma a narcissist brings. It is of course unconscious, but unconscious wounds and pains can often attract unconscious experiences until they are healed. In this sense, the future manipulations and narcissistic abuse we suffer when with a narcissist are due to some deeply buried wound which has its roots in the collective psyche and 'wound of the soul.' There is a natural part of self which is bound for suffering, due to being human. Like the seed which only knows darkness until it finally evolves and sprouts above the earth, we all have lessons, trials and tribulations which are essential aspects to our unique journey. The intense sexual attraction one feels for a true narcissist can be seen equating to this.

2. *Desire for codependency*: If you have low self-esteem, lack confidence or are simply steered towards codependency narcissists can be extremely attractive. They appeal to you because they appear 'on it,' as if they have everything together. They also give the impression that they are strong, centered and sincere- qualities which are highly ap-

pealing to a sensitive and submissive nature. You can truly believe the narcissist will provide for your needs, further being the rock and gem you desire. In general, codependency is a natural part of life however its degree depends on your own insecurities and sense of independence. Many codependents people please and sacrifice themselves in some way for others. Due to a narcissist's hidden nature (which you only discover much further down the line or once you are already married), this makes them attractive and magnetic. You literally magnetize them into your orbit and vice versa based on both of your individual- yet highly different- attitudes and beliefs towards intimacy and connection. At first it appears like you are on the exact same wave, however down the line you realize that your desire for codependency or simply a shared and mutual relationship is in polarity to the narcissist's intentions.

3. *Seduction*: Narcissists are skilled seductors and seductresses. They have mastered the art of manipulation and furthermore are comfortably integrated into that role. Seduction is not just sexual, it is also mental, emotional and psychological.

They can be incredible listeners and provide a false sense of security, allowing you to believe they have your best interests at heart through their patience and communicative abilities. Narcissists also have alluring qualities and use flattery, self-disclosure and vulnerability to entice you into a seductive attraction. Because you are none the wise, this false pretense is incredibly stimulating and can form the basis of your relationship; until you learn their true personality. But this may already be once you are married, unfortunately. If not and you are lucky enough to still be in the dating stage, or know someone who is and don't want them to make the same mistakes you did, being aware of this can be the key to your immediate and long lasting happiness!

4. *Idealization*: Narcissists can be very accomplished, successful, powerful, multi- talented and socially attained, and they can also have lots of achievements which portray them in a favorable light. There can be a strong sense of idealism, further meaning the narcissist is presented as the ultimate or exemplary human being. Regardless of whether you lack personal confidence and self- es-

teem, are prone to codependency, place high importance on social status, or view success and achievement as a form of power; the 'worldly wins' of an egotistical narcissistic are something many idealize. Power, boldness, courage and strength are all the 'light self' of the narcissist who has made a name for themselves, or achieved some form of greatness in the physical world. This is of course a mask, however until you learn their true deep- set narcissism the persona they have created can be extremely attractive and appealing. It is best to memorize the red flags as if they are the Quran, Bhagavad Gita or Bible.

5. *Familiarity*: Unfortunately we carry many wounds with us into adulthood. This means that there can be deep familiarity with narcissists we are attracted to. Many people have narcissistic parents or grandparents so their ways and attitudes become a normal part of life. Even if we don't agree with them, we still accept and tolerate them; thus allowing them into our reality. This has an unconscious yet powerful effect on our inner currents. Chemistry is often signified by some deep and indescribable bond. Your chemistry with

a narcissist can be so appealing that the hidden aspects of consciousness contributing to your attraction maintain hidden for a very long time. During the dating stage, there will always be some sense of comfort, like you have known them from another life or have an unexplainable bond. Unlucky- as this 'soulmate illusion' is in fact a karmic bond where you inevitably get hurt, suffer at the expense of their manipulations and non- compassion, and learn the personal lessons the hard way. Still, it is an undeniable bond and one which does involve a deep connection and sense of familiarity. With the right wisdom, knowledge and guidance you can always come out stronger and wiser.

6. *Need for companionship*: The need for companionship is a basic human desire which drives us all. It is not even human, but animalistic; a drive and necessity present within all species and living organisms. We are born inherently social, creatures which naturally gravitate towards paths of family, community and society. Intimacy and togetherness feel like something that can be provided due to the false charm in the dating and getting to know stages. Like with the 'hidden wounds' and

subsequent magnetism expressed in sexual attraction, your lack of awareness as to their true colors can be majorly appealing if you have any karmic or self- evolutionary lesson which need to come to light. Remember, life is a journey and inevitably involves hardship, pain and suffering. There will always be chances for growth and testing cycles to grow stronger from, integrating the new found wisdom and maturity to be a better you. Your initial attraction for a narcissist and all they have to bring is one of these.

What they Get Attracted To

Anything pure and natural! Any and all beautiful and attractive qualities are on the narcissist's magnetic radar. Let's look at these at face value.

- Intelligence.
- Intellect.
- Being empathetic and compassionate.
- Having humanitarian interests.
- Showing heart.
- Openness.

- Emotional maturity.
- Friendliness and a love for life.
- Positive mental attitude.
- Spirit- an open and happy spirit.
- Success and achievements.
- Hierarchy or societal place on the 'social ladder.'
- Resources- materialistic blessings or achievements.
- Unique talents, gifts and abilities.
- A genuine care for others, animals and the world.
- Shyness and insecurities.
- Someone easily shapeable.
- Inner beauty.
- External beauty and someone they can 'show off.'

Because there are so many elements to the narcissist's personality they can always find some unique trait, gift or aspect of you to cling on to and use as a tool for their narcissistic motivations further down the line. They can easily get attracted to shyness, insecurities and someone 'weaker' or less mature and aged who may be easily molded or manipulated; just as easy as they could choose someone more secure and established within themselves, either with some real physical achievements and successes or some unique strength, positive quality and social status or perceived hierarchy.

Furthermore, humanitarian interests, being genuinely concerned about the well- being and welfare of others, empathy, compassion, morality, kindness, genuinity, sincerity, warm- heartedness and inner beauty are all qualities which a narcissist looks out for. Being aware of the *red flags* are things to be mindful of and can help greatly if you suspect that you may be attracted to a narcissist.

Red Flags

Self- centeredness

Possibly the most profound red flag is a narcissist's self-centeredness. During the dating stage this will show in many different ways, through body language, passing moments of eye contact, and their general demeanour, words and beliefs. It is virtually impossible to hide their self- centeredness and this is a major red flag of their narcissistic nature.

Arrogance

Moments of real and extreme arrogance will always shine through when first getting to know your narcissist. They may attempt to mask it with clever words, a self- righteous and 'holy' attitude, and a charm and wit which they believe excuses them, however the truth remains that their inner and deep-set arrogance is a key warning sign for their true personality to come.

Bragging and need for Admiration

Bragging will be common when you are dating, even when they pull out all the moves to be perceived as charming, attractive and intelligent. Their inner need for admiration and attention is not like the normal person's basic human desire or survival need for connection and attention. Instead of focusing on themselves and their gifts, talents and abilities they will focus on others in a way to help them shine. Comparison is used as a tool in their methods and there is a strong sense of putting themselves on a pedestal. The need for adoration is strong.

Entitlement

One red flag which may not be so obvious but is still a clear sign is your dating partner's sense of entitlement. Regardless of what they are speaking about, whether it be family situations, friendships or something in your immediate environment, there will always be a clear sense of self- entitlement. The key clue here is that they show little to no appreciation and speak with an 'arrogant confidence' when referring to anything they perceive to own, or be worthy of.

Self- Righteousness

Like with entitlement- self- righteousness is another clear sign that you are dating a narcissist. Other associated signals to be conscious of: smugness, lack of empathy, superiority, hypocrisy, smugness, lack of morality, belittlement of others.

Belittling and 'Negative Speak'

Finally, talking bad of others is a key red flag that you are about to enter a codependent- narcissistic relationship. Whereas most people lift others up, see the light in others for inspiration and a sense of oneness, community and unity, or generally just have helpful, kind and productive things to say; the narcissist will engage in frequent negative speak and even belittling or slandering. They may just slip it into the conversation in a manipulative way with some clear hidden false intention or motivation, or their personality may be more apparent and they more upfront. Either way, the innate need to speak bad of others and put others down is a red flag to be mindful of.

Signs You Have Narcissist Victim Syndrome

There is a difference between being a victim and playing victim. You are a victim because you have to suffer the abuse and narcissistic ways of your narcissist partner. However, *playing victim* ultimately takes away your personal power. Shifting responsibility is not beneficial for anyone and by choosing to cling on to this reality, you inevitably adopt a type of syndrome associated with your feelings and experiences of victimhood.

Before going into the signs and manifestations of Narcissist Victim Syndrome (NVS) first let's explore what it means to *be* a victim of narcissistic abuse. Please note this will only be present and occur further down the line into your relationship, perhaps even years later or once you are already settled into married life.

Victims of Narcissistic Abuse:-

- Suffer directly at the hands and will of narcissistic partners. They recognize what is occurring from a grounded and self- aware level, viewing the narcissist exactly as they are. Self- awareness here is key.

- Suffer indirectly at the hands and will of narcissists. Victims see the narcissist's behaviour and intentions for what they are and realize that they are a target and supply for their partner's personality. There is no sense of *choosing* to adopt a victim role, they unfortunately naturally become a victim from the narcissist's actions.

- Attempt to take back their personal power and sovereignty. Instead of 'playing' into the hands and intentions of the narcissist true victims of abuse will always try to retain their own independence and personal integrity.

- Try to heal or help their partner in some way. Whereas those with NVS may lower their vibration to that of their partner's, people who are genuinely victims to narcissistic abuse will attempt to *raise* their partner's vibration.

- Have a lot of patience, understanding, compassion and wisdom. They may use their perception, insight and own inner strength and personal integrity to transcend the patterns of narcissistic abuse.

- Make a conscious decision to not suffer, even if this fails and they suffer directly or indirectly as a result of the narcissist's abuse. They understand they have a choice and try to remain strong, regardless of the circumstances presented to them.

- Walk on eggshells or sacrifice their own mental and emotional health to appease, or please their abuser. They suffer actual psychological turmoil and put aside their own needs, wants and desires for their narcissistic partner.
- Attempt to protect their partner in some way or even allow themselves to be gaslighted. There is always an underlying current of wanting them and the relationship to change for the better.

Narcissistic Victim Syndrome and Why it is Unhealthy for Your Well- Being

Narcissistic Victim Syndrome, however, is consciously (or subconsciously) "lowering your vibe" to match the energy of the narcissist. Being a victim of narcissistic abuse can be a very serious and traumatic experience. The energy, projections and harmful intentions of the narcissist linger in your conscious mind and energy body for quite some time. What is the energy body? The energy body is the part of self responsible for the whole person- all of you. It is your emotions, memories, beliefs, thoughts, impressions, persona, psyche, character and personality. It is also your soul essence, the core of your being. Victims of narcissistic abuse suffer severely at the hands of narcissists. Yet, NVS is slightly different.

The key difference is *choice*. You have great power to take back your life and not play to the narcissist's games! Fortunately there are many ways to heal from NVS and transcend the recurring patterns of behavior. Let's look at some of these at face value.

- Therapy
- Self- healing
- Meditation
- Boundary strengthening
- Sound therapy
- Neuro- linguistic programming
- Counselling
- Nature therapy
- Spending more time with friends and family
- Immersing yourself in a passion or hobby

Narcissistic Abuse Syndrome (NAS) is different to NVS, however. Whereas NVS is taking on the role of victim and therefore giving away your power, NAS is recognizing the role of the abuser (the narcissist) and giving yourself the self- love and acceptance needed to heal.

Narcissistic Abuse Syndrome: What is it?

Narcissistic Abuse Syndrome is the deep array of psychological abuse one suffers from a narcissist. It is not as random or sporadic as narcissistic displays in passing or from a friend of a friend or acquaintance; but it is usually suffered when in a relationship with someone, or if you have formed a deep bond over a longer period of time. There is an element of karmic interplay involved in NAS, as the sufferer always unconsciously enters into some energetic and karmic entanglement.

If you are divorcing or taking the steps to divorce then you most likely have NAS or suffer from some of its symptoms. The symptoms are many and there are many sociopathic and psychopathic tendencies displayed by the narcissist. NAS is arguably one of the most extreme forms of narcissistic abuse, or narcissism in its optimum. It is essentially a condition triggered by being in a "warzone" with a narcissist who continuously seeks to take control and command over you. Your thoughts, beliefs, emotions, will, mind and whole being are no longer your own. You are instead 'owned' by the narcissist and entrapped in their games.

It is an often indescribable attack on the spirit, psyche, soul and personal identity. Being a sufferer of NAS can leave you feeling abused and with some form of PTSD. Your psyche is under constant assault and name calling, belittling, mind games and gaslighting are present and extreme.

Gaslighting

To start, if you suffer from Narcissistic Abuse Syndrome you will almost certainly be gaslighted. The narcissist will attempt to erase you from their existence in a way which makes you question your own sanity, intentions, abilities and self- worth. Your self- esteem will plummet and you may suffer with severe depression or anxiety. Gaslighting is making you question your reality. You could be the most selfless, sincere, genuine, kind, giving, patient, compassionate and empathetic of beings, yet with NAS you will doubt all of these qualities.

There is also a question of being believed. It can be very hard to stand strong in your own truth and clarity as the narcissist will attempt to distort truths and "tell stories" to some of your closest friends and family.

Emotional Abuse

The emotional abuse suffered at the hands of a narcissist is on par with the psychological and mental abuse when dealing with a psychopath or sociopath. They use language in specific ways with intentions of capturing and imprisoning your mind and will. *Emotional manipulation* and all it's connotations is most extreme in NAS. In fact, if someone was asked to picture the most severe forms of emotional manipulation, the characteristic of Narcissistic Abuse Syndrome would be the optimal.

Deep and Severe Manipulation

Connected to emotional abuse is the deep and severe levels of manipulation present. Referring back to the use of language previously mentioned; mental, emotional and psychological manipulation will be apparent, frequent and often. The victim and sufferer will not know where to turn or how to escape from such extreme exertions of manipulation. Friends, family and mutual acquaintances will even be turned and swayed. One key thing to know is that narcissists are incredible story- tellers. They will use your thoughts, desires, possessions, self- esteem, willpower and own strength reserves for their own gain.

Betrayal

Narcissists are experts at betrayal. There is no limit to the amount of pain, suffering and deception a narcissist can exhibit. Furthermore they simply don't care. They lack empathy to the point of sadism and are happy to intentionally inflict deep trauma and betrayal on those who love and care for them. Linked to this is the aspect of bullying. You may not only be lied about and betrayed in this sense, but also bullied, threatened and made to feel severely weak or inferior through words and speech. This is a complete betrayal of your trust, of your heart and your sincerity, and can further leave you feeling completely isolated, victimized and traumatized.

Psychopathic and Sociopathic Behaviors

Extreme narcissists such as those who cause NAS often display sociopathic and psychopathic tendencies. A prime example is the following: a narcissist would run you over and tell you off for being in their way. They will endlessly complain about you being in their way and make you feel bad for being run over! A sociopath would run you over, stop to smile or smirk at the pain and destruction they have caused, and then scold you for being in their way; all whilst being silently smug and happy at the chaos. Finally, a psychopath will do everything in their power to run you over, going out of their way intentionally to make sure that the utmost chao was caused. They will not only blame you for being in their way, but they would laugh; even backtracking to make sure they haven't missed a toe or fingertip.

This may seem like an extreme analogy, yet it portrays the type of energy and hidden motivations present in narcissists, sociopaths and psychopaths. Although narcissists may seem like the less extreme one out of the three, the main point is that they still show signs and actions- behaviors of socio- and psychopaths. Quite simply, Narcissistic Abuse Syndrome is as severe as they come.

Zero Empathy

It has already been mentioned but it still can't be stressed enough. Narcissists have zero empathy, meaning that they also feel no remorse for their evil deeds. They are egocentric, never apologize, don't know how to apologize; are expert story- tellers, present themselves as having high morals, are untruthful and manipulative, have superficial charm and an imposed sense of (false/ fake) social grace or philosophy, and feign like, love or care to get what they want. They can make themselves appear as the hero with superior morality when in reality they are evil, heartless and cold inside. An extreme narcissist truly has no shame or problem with ruining someone else's life.

Post- Traumatic Stress Disorder (PTSD)

Finally, one of the major results of being on the receiving end of Narcissistic Abuse Syndrome is the development of PTSD and related symptoms. It may be easy to want to shrug off the severity of NAS, see the victims or sufferers as dramatic or attention- seeking, or generally downplay the situation for what it is; however, those who suffer with real cases of Narcissistic Abuse Syndrome go through real psychological, mental and emotional abuse.

Some of the consequences of NAS in relation to PTSD can include:-

- Nightmares, flashbacks or recurring memories.
- Physical- emotional reactions and responses.
- Trauma, both on the surface and deeply buried.
- Avoidance of other people and a detrimental desire for excessive solitude.

- Intrusive thoughts, emotions, memories and manipulations.
- Negative and anxiety- ridden mindset.
- Negative and destructive/ harmful self- image and image about the world.
- Isolation and extreme detachment from friends, family and peers.
- Insomnia, anxiety and stress disorders.
- Fear to be oneself. Irrational and delusional fears.
- Extremely low self- worth, self- esteem and confidence.

Of course, these are some of the more extreme cases of being a sufferer of NAS, however they are still able to show up. Usually these symptoms and PTSD related tendencies present themselves over a longer period of time, once the chance to heal and begin a path to recovery has passed (or is in later stages).

Chapter 2: MARRIAGE AND
THE NARCISSIST

5 Things to Look For in the
Narcissist's View of Marriage

Wouldn't it be a wonderful world if everyone was honest and had some written message on their person making clear of their intentions and motivations... Unfortunately this is not the case. Narcissists do not interact with others with a pin badge stating, *"I enjoy psychotic games and manipulating others. If you want a crazy. chaotic and profound self- exploration journey which involves suffering but deep and life- changing lessons; apply within!"* If we knew this was their game all along we could at least make the choice ourselves, detaching from the emotions and desires for intimacy and accepting that this person may be best for a fling, brief love affair or way to heal and express our sexuality!

Yet in terms of marriage and partnership, the games and deceptions of a narcissist do not make for the best partner. In fact, there is no *partner*ship present at all; perhaps only in fleeting moments. Partnership implies unity, harmony, and a mutual respect, trust and connection. All a narcissist has to offer is mind games, suffering, confusion and oppression. It can be highly oppressive living and being with a narcissist as they don't like to see you happy, thriving or succeeding in your own personal goals, dreams and aspirations. (We explored this earlier.)

Before going into the 8 reasons why a narcissist gets married, let's first discover 5 things to watch out for.

Number 1: The Need to Control

Narcissists are extremely controlling. They see their partner as a target or supply for their deep- seated manipulations and need to control. Fortunately you can spot this tendency early on, creating better boundaries and inner strength. It can be more difficult once you are already enticed and wrapped around their little finger, but if you can remain strong and centered from the start then there shouldn't be a problem with recognizing this sign that you are with a narcissist.

This control reflects into many areas. It may be the clothes you wear, your beliefs, your daily habits and actions, your likes and dislikes, and your holistic identity and sense of self. Whichever the expression, you are simply not allowed to be you or be free to make your own life choices.

Number 2: Emotion- Phobia!

Quite simply, narcissists are terrified of emotions. This is not in reference to manipulation or using negative and harmful emotional intents to cause pain or chaos, but it is talking about real and sincere emotions and connection. Unlike in normal relationships where love, care and affection are prevalent, narcissists are incapable of true intimacy and subsequently see marriage as a way to exert their dominance and emotional superiority. Of course, the narcissist is not in any way, shape or form emotionally superior- however they see themselves as better than you in some way. This is because of the distorted view that emotions and vulnerability are weak and inferior.

Earlier on you will recognize the need to use emotions to control, manipulate, dominate and suppress and will further realize that these personality traits are a precourse to married   life.

Number 3: A Fragmented Family History?

There will always be some aspect of childhood trauma, repressions and family stories with your narcissistic partner. Most people see childhood or family related wounds as a way to self- develop, heal and transcend wounds and pains brought from childhood. Yet a narcissist is so afraid of vulnerability and looking to the core of themselves that the patterns and wounds brought from childhood will show their ugly face in your relationship. Your partner will use projection as a means to hide from their own issues, also masking their inner securities and wounds with negative and hurtful displays, words and behaviors.

In terms of what they look for, your partner essentially uses you as their scapegoat, perpetuating the cycles they are yet to heal.

Number 4: Projection: You As their Mirror

You are essentially their mirror. Like with projecting their family traumas and childhood wounds, the narcissists perceives you as their mirror or shield to their own ignorance. Many things which require patience, understanding and compassion; a desire to help and heal one another, are instead met with projection. Imagine throwing a ball at a wall. Regardless of how many times the ball hits the wall, it will always bounce back. The ball is symbolic of the narcissist's intentions, motivation and inner turmoil and the wall is you. You are simply their shield and structure to bounce off, and keep their games in play. Regardless of the negative trait, situation, story or (destructive) intention, the narcissist will always see you as someone to stand by their side or in front of them to take their 'stuff'.

Number 5: Insecurities Masked As Arrogance (and other less than favorable qualities)

You will know you are with a narcissist when their deeply buried insecurities start to come to light. They will always be masked as arrogance, a false sense of superiority, self-centeredness, an inflated ego, and other less desirable personality traits. Real displays of vulnerability, raw emotion, and low feeling or moods which are natural and a part of our humanity will never be shown. Wounds, traumas, doubts, fears, and general self- discovery or self-development are all covered by a need to appear the best, all together, omniscient and forcefully superior. There is no sense of room and space for healing and in the narcissist's eye they are already perfect. They want you to believe they are perfect too, and anything which threatens their sense of self- created status is met with abuse, manipulation or projection- like tactics.

In the narcissist's eye, you are less smart, less accomplished, less capable and less deserving, in all areas of life.

8 Reason Why a Narcissist Gets Married

This brings us onto why a narcissist gets married. This section may be heard to understand and comprehend, as; let's face it, narcissism is a pretty severe and distorted personality to embody. But the truth will set you free and hopefully further prevent a future marriage or relationship with a narcissist.

A Scapegoat

Unfortunately, you are their scapegoat. Like in the signs and things to watch out for, a narcissist sees you as their mirror to project all their stuff on. You will be blamed for all of their own wrongdoings, judged and persecuted for the narcissist's mistake, faults, and negative traits. This is how narcissists fundamentally view marriage; they see their partner as a tool for shifting blame and passing responsibility. The sad truth is that they need this. They need to have someone in their life, hence why they choose to get married. Once they have found someone who is enticed by their charm and immersed in their illusions, they have hit the jackpot. The fact that anyone who does not have Narcissistic Personality Disorder is or has capabilities for compassion, kindness, care, intimacy, patience, and a general sense of 'niceness' signifies that they will make the perfect scapegoat.

To Perpetuate their Own Insecurities/ Traumas/ Emotional Wounds

It may seem like something out of a psychological thriller or drama movie, but one of the reasons why a narcissist gets married is to perpetuate their own insecurities, traumas and wounds. Remember that narcissists have some deep vulnerabilities which they are too afraid to admit. Narcissists can live their whole lives in states of inner depression, chaos and turmoil, and with further repressions and unresolved wounds and pains; without ever healing or transcending from them. Their narcissism is simply a cover and a shield to hide them from their own wounds. Like with anything in life, we are social and family- oriented creatures. (Yes, even narcissists!) This means that they need someone to bounce off, be with as a support system and mirror. Of course, the narcissist will never change or even wish to heal or transcend their narcissistic ways, but they need someone all the same. You will be their rock and gem, just unfortunately in a way which drains you, depletes you, and leaves you feeling psychologically and mentally abused.

To Keep their Illusions Intact

Like with the previous point narcissists get married to keep their illusions intact. They need you to stay fooled and enticed in their games and manipulations. The saying there is "support or power in numbers" applies here. In marriage, the narcissist receives your love and support which further empowers them and keeps their narcissistic ways in a sense of acceptance. If there is no support, then there is no acceptance. Something cannot exist without the energy, awareness and thumbs up from people. It is we human beings who create and shape reality as we know it. This is one of the key reasons why a narcissist gets married, because they know that their illusions will only survive and thrive through the support of another. Again, you become like their rock or gem. This support may be unconscious or based on you being fooled and stuck in their games, however it is still a green light.

For Peers and Colleagues

What better way to keep one's social illusions of charm and eloquence in play then to have a level- headed, normal and sincere partner on their arm? Having a husband or wife is the cherry on top of the cake to a narcissist, and also the foundation which keeps their personality and self- created identity at play. To peers and colleagues the narcissist appears normal and even kind, wise and beautiful (in an inner beauty sense) when they have a sane partner by their side. Their partner provides a justification, grounding and acceptance. The narcissist also knows that any moments of their narcissistic personality which may come to light will always be supported, backed up and justified through their partner's compassion and love. It is like you (the husband or wife) perpetuates and makes their innate narcissism OK and acceptable; they know that you will always have their back and make their shadow look like shine. This is because this is what a real partnership and marriage looks like, you are supposed to support your partner and be there for them in times of need. Yet, it is not reciprocated and leaves you clinging onto the idea and false reality that your partner is charming and is capable of a real social grace, kindness and companionship. When you are alone again, you will once again be the target of their games and abuse.

For their Sense of Success: Self Identity and Appearance

Furthermore they need a partner for their success, self-identity and appearance. Their professional and personal life are fuelled by your love and sanity. Companionship and intimacy are a natural and fundamental part of life and the narcissist knows this- even if they can't display real intimacy and companionship themselves. They hide behind you and your favorable beautiful qualities, always making them appear in a positive light. In fact, their self-identity and public or professional/ personal persona depends on this. If you were to withdraw your support, who would they be? They could be exposed in their real character, or their hidden intentions and motivations could be brought to the surface. Marriage to a sane, sincere and non- narcissistic partner is the perfect shield.

'The Charm Illusion'

Most people would not choose a partner or life long companion if they knew they would be psychologically and emotionally abusive, manipulative and holistically speaking lacking in such empathy. So this is the precise reason why a narcissist needs a marriage partner. Who would want to be married to a narcissist and enter into such a formal and long- standing agreement? The answer is no one- no one would willingly or consciously choose this. It all therefore comes down to the charm illusion, the illusion from the start of your connection that your partner really is charming, decent and sincere. If their husband or wife sees them as beautiful, kind and worthy of a loving and supportive marriage, why wouldn't others see them as worthy in other aspects of life? A narcissist depends on the support and love of friends, peers and colleagues, so having yours is the first and main step. You are like the anchor, cement and seed all in one. Without you, the narcissist is nothing. *"The charm illusion"* is essentially the delusions and harmful stories your partner can keep through your own acceptance and compassionate, yet self- detrimental, support.

To Be in Control

Like with the things to watch out for, a narcissist needs to be in control. In other words, they *need someone to control.* It may be a hard truth to accept but you are ultimately their plaything. Without someone to control, command or order the narcissist's illusions begin to break down. Without their illusions their world falls apart, so they need this false sense of superiority and dominance. Regardless of whether it is something small or something big, any sense of being in control is fuel to their fire. The traits and tendencies of the narcissist personality are all enhanced and expanded through having someone to bounce off and control. If you are not cooperative and present in their games and (often sadistic) intentions then how would they maintain their illusion of control, or 'having it all together?' The truth is that the narcissist is not all together, in any way, shape or form. It is their marriage partner's compliance which allows it.

To Never have to Heal

One of the main and arguably most significant reasons as to why a narcissist gets married is because they never have to heal when they have someone to bounce off and project all their own 'stuff' onto. You are their scapegoat, mirror, shield, rock, gem, projection wall, and foundation all in one! Any and all unresolved traumas, represent wounds, past pains, sadistic and narcissistic traits and characteristics, and personal issues all become accepted and integrated once a narcissist enters marriage. Most people do the work before entering into a partnership as they realize that they should be the best version of themselves before committing to someone. Many and most people don't want to project their unresolved things in a companionship, and for this reason alone the idea of never having to heal or better themselves for both their partner and their own self is unspeakable. Healing and self-development are a natural part of life.

However, to the narcissist marriage is a means of escape. They can escape from their past, their wounds, their narcissism and their often 'evil' and sadistic intentions; through the presence and cover of a life partner. They are incapable of having a healthy, intimate and cooperative or supportive relationship and the lack of empathy and compassion is too prevalent to overlook. Even if you are strong beyond belief, you will still be the sufferer in the marriage due to the narcissist's ability to break your heart over and over. Their own denial, repression and inability to heal becomes your unhealedness.

Narcissistic Cruelty, Whilst Being Kind To Everyone Else!

The best way to approach this topic is to look at the Greek mythological story of *Narcissus*. Narcissus was son of the river God Cephissus and nymph Liriope. Many women fell in love with Narcissus, yet he only showed disdain, indifference and neglect. He enjoyed being admired and sought after but could never reciprocate others' affections or positively expressed affections and emotions, further causing much pain to many. His *narcissism* eventually led to his demise.

This story from Greek mythology ultimately sums up why narcissists are so cruel. They need to appear kind to others to keep their illusions in play, as we have discussed and explored throughout, however they also need someone to project and target. The cruelty you suffer is, unfortunately, the result of the love and adoration you feel; all brought on and developed from their initial charm. It is a very sad and often harsh reality to accept, yet the more you accept it and perhaps integrate the lessons from the story of Narcissus, the better you are able to heal and move on from the pain. Like Narcissus, narcissists only love themselves as reflected in the eyes of others; so, in other words, the love you have for them sustains them. In reality and deep down, narcissists do not like or love themselves at all! They may actually dislike themselves immensely. This is due to their inflated egos, self- flattery, arrogance and self- denial, which are all known by the subconscious and unconscious mind even if not integrated into the persona or core personality.

In truth, narcissists have a unique *self- loathing* which is very hard to admit and impossible to heal from. The cruelty and mental, emotional and psychological abuse you suffer are all a projection of their own insecurities and self- loathing. Although it may appear like quite the opposite through their powerful self- confidence and self- assurity, narcissists are deeply fearful to take a true look at themselves. Emotionally they are dead inside, lifeless and incapable of intimacy or companionship. Mentally, they are yet to heal from their own wounds and inner demons.

Your narcissist partner is hungry for validation, admiration and approval because they secretly cannot provide this for them self, regardless of how strong their delusions and false images may present themselves.

The ultimate result of this projected cruelty and inner pain is a real unappreciation and neglect of your love, care and support; and an alienation of you and everything you stand for. The more patience, compassion and special attention you give, the more you are likely to be on the receiving end of their abusive and sadistic projections. Love is met with hate, compassion is met with uncaring, and all of your attempts for companionship, intimacy and partnership are responded to like Narcissus with his many admirers. Other people, however, receive kindness; or at least a fake and 'put on' sense of kindness, because they are so insecure and vulnerable inside that they need the support and validation of others. If they were truly alone in the world with no outside support or "friendship," they would have to actually stop and look at their own reflection- and subsequent inner demons. So, you become their main target and primary victim.

"The Hatred Illusion"

The big question and the root of many psychological topics of discussion. How can someone appear to hate you so strongly whilst being incapable of letting you go? Being a target of narcissistic 'hatred' is a confusing experience, mainly because they don't actually hate you yet project all of their own insecurities and vulnerabilities. The hatred may appear as real hatred however it is not. You are simply their wall to shield their own pain. For this reason it is very hard, if not impossible and unseen, for the narcissist to be the one to let their partner go. If they have found someone they can use as a mirror to project back all their own issues, unless you end it you are almost certainly in it for the long haul.

It can be soul- shattering to give your all to a narcissist and be continuously reminded that they will never change, despite your faith and clinging onto the memories of how they were when you first met. Each time you feel like you've finally made progress- and after expending all your energy and more- they slap you down with speech, energy and actions which leave you utterly confused, hurt and betrayed. It is as if they truly hate you to the core of your soul, and on a level they do. Soul is the innermost essence of self. It is the part of someone which transcends this physical and three dimensional reality, the deepest and sincerest level of being possible to describe with the human mind. On a soul level, you are the greatest teacher for the narcissist, here to show them what compassion, companionship and unconditional love is. The narcissist is also your greatest teacher.

This is the fundamental reason why your partner's actions, words and ways may seem as pure venom and hatred, because in a sense; they are. They despise all you on a real and deep level because you are everything they cannot be. Unlike in personalities and people who have varying elements of light and dark, shine and shadow, a narcissist is truly incapable of change or *seeing the light.* They attack all your beautiful qualities and grow increasingly more narcissistic and hateful at your sincere displays of empathy, patience, kindness and compassion. They long to be loving inside, as love is the foundation of all sentient beings. Yet, they are so entwined with their own insecurities, self- hatred and unhealed wounds that it almost impossible to transcend their ways in their lifetime. The issues here run deep.

Of course, why can't they see a counsellor, receive therapy or begin a journey of self- healing and development; you may be wondering? I think you already know the answer to this. Narcissists aren't *normal*, there is nothing normal about them. This is not saying that we non- narcissists are better than them or all shine, and no shadow. It is, however, referring to the fact that narcissists are incapable of seeing their shadow and learning from it, or seeking to overcome it and heal their own repetitive cycles and behaviors. Where normal people would recognize the imperfection of life and need to better oneself, a narcissist is unable to do so. They believe they are perfect, whole and healed even when their true self knows deep down that they are not. Their narcissistic ways have already become their persona, a self- created character which is virtually impossible to escape from. Narcissists are their own worst enemy.

So in terms of being in a relationship with a narcissist this signifies that you are already doomed from the start. Unlike in true relationships and companionships where both partners are open to learning, growing and evolving together, your 'narcissistic other' uses you as a mirror, wall or shield to their arrogance, imposed dominance, manipulations and hidden insecurities. You ultimately become their life support.

It is also significant to look at the different *types* of narcissist in relation to the apparent hatred you receive.

Types of Narcissists

Introvert or Closet

Introvert or 'closet' narcissists are the type of narcissists who appear moody, down or depressed as the result of their innate narcissism. They may not be in the spotlight or like to be center stage, yet they still embody the narcissistic traits which make them selfish, egocentric and domineering. These types of narcissists use their hidden personality traits to entice you into feeling sorry for them or wanting to 'lower your vibe.' Their depression, low moods and generally down and unsatisfied outlook on life are due to their personality traits, and these are used to manipulate you and keep you in a state of suffering.

Introvert or closet narcissists are still extremely manipulative and selfish, however it may not be so in your face as other types. Still, they use their masked depression (which is purely a result of their own doing and character deficits) to control you and cause pain, always leaving you feeling guilty or sorry for them. Their innate selfishness, arrogance and lack of compassion or empathy, or care for anyone other than themselves, keeps you in a detrimental cycle where they are always smiling on the inside whereas you are in a state of constant suffering. Although they may appear down or depressed, these narcissists in fact get their kicks of your suffering and despair. They, unfortunately, feel genuine joy and satisfaction at your unhappiness.

Malignant

Malignant narcissists are one of the worst types of narcissists you will ever come across. They are soul destroyers, wandering through life finding their next victims and new stream of lives to ruin. They are malicious, cruel, highly manipulative and hostile, with a real spiteful and poisonous nature. They can destroy through their words, actions or hidden motivations and usually have some sort of hidden and 'behind the scenes' plot. These types of narcissists are the types that would take you to court and attempt to take you for everything you have, even when they have already stolen off you or ruined your life in some way. They make up lies and rumors and spread hateful, hurtful or destructive stories about you. Their intentions may be many, but the goal is always to receive personal gain at complete dismissal, and often belittlement or ridicule, to your life and self. Your nature and beautiful qualities can be so severely distorted that even your closest friends and family could start to question your intentions and actions.

Malignant narcissists are the most hateful and venomous types of people you could ever come across. There is nothing 'normal' or sane about them and if you ever have the misfortune to be a victim or target of one, you will start to evaluate whether you have in fact been dealing with a real psychopath or sociopath. Furthermore, these narcissists can actually be very dangerous, taking their evil intentions so far as to cause real harm. They are, very simply, cruel.

Extreme

Extreme narcissists are the narcissistic characters you will most likely be dealing with. Unless you are dealing with a closet or malignant narcissist all narcissists are extreme, as narcissism is an extreme type of personality. Selfishness, a real lack of empathy, egocentricity, the need for adoration and to be loved, and a deep seated arrogance, ignorance and self- centeredness are all optimally embodied in the normal narcissist. They can be seen as extreme because their behaviors and attitudes are pretty destructive and questionable. When in a work or social situation, you can really observe just how narcissistic they are. The need to be in the spotlight, at the expense of others, and outshine everyone in a rather 'wow' (negative wow) way is apparent. So is their response if they are ever questioned in a public or social situation.

In personal or love/ romantic relationships, extreme narcissists portray the traits expressed throughout previous chapters. Narcissistic personality disorder can be viewed as an extreme personality disorder as a narcissist is completely disconnected from everything decent, moral and humane. Real emotions, situations and daily interactions are virtually non existent and are often replaced with mean, spiteful or bullyish behaviors and scenarios. Manipulation, emotional blackmail and mind games are present, and any attempt to bring love, intimacy or kindness to your relationship is met with further narcissistic responses. In short, extreme narcissists can be a nightmare.

Chapter 3: DIVORCING A NARCISSIST

*"It may be difficult at first but
divorcing a narcissist is worth it."*

I sn't this a statement you tell yourself every day!? It plays in your mind like a mantra, the self- affirmation reminding you that going in the right direction will be worth it in the end. It should be so easy- why stay with someone who has no empathy, care or kindness towards you and who wants to see you suffer? Yet it is not a easy as it seems, hence why you need to repeat statements such as this.

This is one thing that many people don't tell you when taking the steps to divorce a narcissist. You need mantras or affirmation- like statements to keep you on course, re-mind you that this really is in your best interests, and that it will be worth it in the end. The psychological, mental and emotional abuse and trauma you have suffered are real, and regardless of how many times you have been gaslighted, or made to appear crazy, in the wrong or los-ing the plot, you know the truth in the core of your cells.

Being with a narcissist is completely detrimental to your health.

Luckily there are many steps which can be taken. A covert narcissist is exactly this- covert; still in the shadows of their own manipulations, delusions and shady- hurtful character. They are not (yet) in the open or publicly acknowledged, and is this because you have not yet made the decision to allow them to be seen in their true light? Taking a stand and *choosing*, with your own free will, inner strength and shear conviction, that you will no longer allow yourself to be abused, victimized or manipulated allows your partner to be seen, and for you to subsequently finally take the steps necessary to be free from their abuse.

Of course, all of this is something you know- so see these words as a reflection of your own psyche and conscious mind telling you exactly how it is. The fact that you are reading this and have chosen, consciously, to align with your true self and leave your narcissistic partner for good implies that you are already well on course. This is confirmation, and you are heading in the right direction! You are strong beyond measure.

Divorcing a Narcissist:
Stop Reacting!

Reaction. Reaction is not the same as response. When you respond to someone or something, you provide a space, wisdom and awareness to connect on a mature and responsible level. Responding allows for authenticity, calmness or thought and clarity in communication. Yet, reacting is something completely different.

The key to your narcissistic partner's success is in your reaction. They need people to become emotionally entwined and engaged with their stories. If there is no reaction then there is no exchange- no one is appeasing or empowering them. Power is a great word to be aware of here. Reaction provides a narcissist's empowerment, or more accurately faulty sense of empowerment. Causing pain, hurt and manipulation to others is *not* empowerment. Regardless, reacting provides the sustenance that a narcissist needs, so the best way to heal and begin your own journey of empowerment is to stop reacting and start responding.

Things to Be Mindful of: How you may be Reacting!

1. Your partner attempts to provoke a reaction and you allow it. Instead of taking a moment to slow down, be calm inside and recognize the intentions of causing destruction, chaos and harm; you play to their manipulations. Thus, a vicious and highly repetitive cycle can begin and continue for hours or even days on end. The key is to detach and not get caught up in their games. It can be easier said than done, however the tips and techniques for effective response below can really help with this.

2. 'Snide remarks.' Expanding from example 1, at this stage your partner should know you very well and therefore know your *triggers*. Snide remarks or specific comments are a very effective way to get a reaction from you and subsequently enable them to continue in their ways.

3. *'Awareness goes where energy flows!'* If you don't give your attention, time or energy to something, how can it perpetuate? The answer is that it can't. The intentions and motivations of your partner require energy and attention, otherwise they are formless.

4. Watch out for the signs. Assuming you have been with your partner for awhile you will know the signs to when they are going to begin their games. If they are bored or displaying signs of frustration, stimulation or boredom this is a sure warning that you will soon become their target for their stimulation. A narcissist needs that 'spark' to feed their egocentricity, self- centeredness and feelings of self- worth. Without it, their illusions start to crumble down and they have no choice but to look within, seek help and ways to change; which are of course very rare for a narcissist.

5. If you feel yourself becoming stressed, anxious, nervous or heated inside, these are sure signs that you are on the verge of a reaction. Unlike in partnerships where narcissism is not present or a key theme, and where most people are allowed a few moments of blowing off steam or showing weakness; in this relationship you are not provided the patience, compassion or support necessary. This means that even when or if your partner does happen to be in a serene, kind or non- narcissistic space you may unfortunately spark them with your own reactive behaviors. It is extremely rare for a true narcissist to see you becoming upset or

worked up on your own accord and not use it as a chance for drama, or further manipulation.

A Deeper Look into Divorce and Reaction

Divorce is a serious thing. The process inevitably means that you have decided to part ways, restart your life and take back your individual resources, belongings and physical necessities. This in itself is a major red flag in a codependent- narcissist relationship! Your partner's entire identity is merged in the reality that he or she can feed off you, use you as their hidden and subtle yet powerful support system, and bounce off your kindness, empathy and positive attributes. So, once you starting responding this destroys their world. They can no longer keep up the facade once you make the decision that their actions are not acceptable. This can *only* happen when you begin to respond.

How to Start Responding

True response begins when you start to slow down and become an observer of both your own thoughts and feelings and your partner's. This is best achieved through *meditation* and *mindfulness*. The significance of these two self- help methods cannot be overlooked. They are both extremely powerful in helping you to live your best life, be free from narcissistic abuse or targetting, and to start responding.

Meditation

Why is engaging in meditation one of the best ways to learn how to respond and thus change the way you perceive and feel about the situation? Because, meditation allows you to *detach* from overactive thoughts and feelings, further becoming the observer. When you observe you are not caught up in the emotions or drama associated with your partner's intentions. You can calm your mind, control your feelings and responses, and feel more peaceful within. Clarity of mind and thought can also result and you generally become more insightful, patient, wise and loving with meditation.

In the final chapter there is some guidance on how to do this if you are new to meditation.

Mindfulness

Linked to meditation is the power of mindfulness. Mindfulness is exactly what the word implies, it allows you to become more mindful or *conscious*. Being conscious simply means embodying a higher awareness and level of integrity. You won't want to react when you start to integrate the lessons and vibration of mindfulness as you will not want to lower yourself to such levels. There is an innate dosage of eloquence, self- respect, grace and personal integrity associated and developed with mindfulness, and your viewpoints and perspectives will change for the better. Any action or behavior of your partner can be met with greater conscious reaction and response. Further, you will start to feel good about the situation, regardless of how testing it is, and will see the positive.

In essence, mindfulness can help you see the light and recognize that your mind is a powerful tool. You are not responsible for your partner's thoughts, behaviors or in/actions, but you do have control over your own.

How to start responding is further continued in the next section.

How to Manage Conflict

Managing conflict is the same if not similar to learning how to respond. When dealing with someone with deeply buried narcissism, you need to know how to respond appropriately and in a way that doesn't cause further harm to yourself. Once again, you are not responsible for the narcissist's energy. You may have spent years being the most patient, loyal, loving and understanding or empathetic partner, yet these qualities are all lost on them. Managing conflict during or after the divorce proceedings should not be viewed as any different.

Please do not make the mistake of thinking that now you are finally free, or soon to be free, that your partner will suddenly 'see sense' or have a heartfelt awakening. They will not. A narcissist will always view you as their scapegoat and wall or mirror to project their stuff onto, so now you are taking the correct steps and working towards your own wellbeing and happiness; they do not want to let go or give you up so easy.

The following steps may seem simple or effortlessly implemented, yet they are not! Narcissists will do everything in their power to maintain their illusion of power, and try to keep you entrapped in their games until it really is all over. So, in order to combat this and manage conflict successfully, do stay committed and completely aligned to the following. They are all necessary for your happiness, peace of mind and success.

1. Patience

The key to your success when going through a divorce or separation is to focus on your own self and personal qualities. The narcissist has spent months, years or even decades (hopefully not!) unwilling to change, so they are not going to start now. This signifies that the only way to get through this and see your own intentions and goals materialized is to stay centered and focused on yourself. Having patience is the first step.

2. Staying Centered: Personal Boundaries!

Maintaining and potentially developing your boundaries is the second major element to this. Boundaries are essential as they keep you *self- aligned, centered* and *con-*

nected to your truth. Without boundaries you may fall prey to your partner's malicious intentions or attempts of sabotage. Nothing and no one can take away your power, and this is something to keep in mind when separating from a narcissist. Actually, don't just keep it in mind; know it within. You hold great personal power and with strong boundaries your mental projections can act as a shield to all of your partner's bs.

3. Kindness, Tolerance & Self- Respect

Above anything else you need to have self- respect. This links with kindness and tolerance, which are both necessary to manage and deal with conflict harmoniously. The self- respect part is the trinity due to the fact that you won't receive much kindness or respect from your partner, unfortunately. However, you should seek to remain kind and tolerant during the process. There is great truth in the validity of the power or law of attraction. We attract, magnetize and harmonize to us what we give out, so any energy or intentions we project we will receive. If you are sending out harmful, hurtful or separation based vibrations- you shall receive more from your partner. In other words, you cannot fight chaos and narcissism with more destruction or ill wishes! Showing kindness and respect, even if in neutral and indifferent civil ways, will allow you to remain sane, clear headed and calm; also enabling you to stay as clear as possible from your partner's detrimental motivations.

4. Being Your Own Best Friend, Lover and Soulmate

To succeed, you need to be your own best friend, lover and soulmate. You need to practice self- love and show up for yourself (because your narcissistic partner isn't going to). Managing conflict is not just about what you can do for the other person or situation as a whole, but it is about what you can do for yourself. Being your best self for you allows you to be your best self for others. Even if your partner is incapable of rationality or niceness, this commitment to being the best version of you still has a positive effect. Subtle energy and intentions are real and showing up for yourself in a way which states that you are self- loving, self- respecting and not going to tolerate anything less than harmonious and ethical cooperation, means that the situation will flow better than if you didn't commit to these things. Your vibe projects outwards also influencing physical reality and the experiences you attract. How divorce or separation proceedings go can all be changed and shaped by your mindset.

5. Gaining Support

The importance of peer, family and friendship support cannot be disregarded when divorcing a narcissist. Your ability to manage conflict is largely tied in with the amount of support you receive. It can be both a coping mechanism and essential aspect to your recovery and conflict resolution. Narcissists thrive off the social support and cooperation of others

How to Deal with a Narcissist in Court

This only applies if you are dealing with an extreme or malignant narcissist who truly wants to gaslight you and destroy your world. As you may have learned by now, there are people like this in existence. Some narcissists really do have zero empathy and enjoy inflicting severe chaos and intended suffering on others. If you find yourself needing to take your ex to court, therefore, it is wise to become knowledgeable on how to do so.

First let's briefly explore the reasons why you would need to beat or expose a narcissist in the court system.

- Financial manipulation, theft or monetary losses as the result of their narcissism.
- Family and domestic disputes with children involved.
- Question of resources, assets, shared business or joint ventures.
- In extreme cases, physical abuse as a devolution of their mental, emotional and psychological abuse inflicted.
- Any consequence of their 'evil' and cruel nature. Remember, malignant narcissists can be truly heartless.

How to deal with a narcissist in court

☐ What you should know: They've found your wound. They have infected your wound with negativity! Your wounds are what feeds them, so find healing and put boundaries up. Focus on yourself and not them. This enables you to stay connected to your story and not dragged into theirs.

☐ Deflect! Deflect their 'evil' (unbelievably sadistic and harmful) intentions. Don't allow them to get into your personal boundaries. Be wise and take preventative measures for your protection. Engaging in some meditative or mindful activity leading up to court can really help with this.

❏ Don't expect them to play fair. Assume the worst case scenarios- put yourself in their shoes and see all perspectives. How would the worst person in the world word things and try and play it? What angles do they have on you? Take a step back and see the big picture, including all the negative, shadow and dark parts. You may be kind, decent and a lovely human being but the narcissist will pick the tiniest negative and amplify it for their own gain (and your destruction). Be in the know and wise.

❏ Recognize their arrogance and misplaced confidence. Remember, the narcissist is feeding and playing off some distorted truths and out of place perspectives. Their reality is made from these distortions and elements which can potentially destroy you and your world. Recognizing that a lot of what they say, perceive and attempt stems from some delusion, illusion or false belief can help you overcome the effects effectively and efficiently.

❏ *Do not try to expose them as a narcissist!* This is vital and crucial to your success. Trying to expose them or label them just looks like 'finger- pointing.' Instead, be humble and actively practice humility, staying centered in your own reality and truth. Trying to expose them in a negative light is essentially attracting negativity to yourself (where awareness goes, energy flows.)

❏ People will be susceptible to kindness and seeing the positive. Respect is given to those who respect others and choose to act with kindness, not engaging in negative talk. Being sophisticated, courteous and completely truthful in your words and dealings ultimately makes you appear as the best version of yourself, and naturally exposes the narcissist.

❏ Adopt the principle: "respond, don't react." Allow him or her to lie and remain calm yourself. Maintaining calm even when the narcissist is blatantly lying or speaking badly about you, trying to represent you in a false light, is the best and most powerful way to get your message across. The words and actions of a narcissist are never on the same page- allow it play out. Allow them to speak untrue. Focus on the facts and actions, as real actions speak louder than any mistruths or manipulations. In other words, do not resist or react to

DR. THERESA J. COVERT

your partner's story and intended mistruths, as the facts will come to light.

❑ Put the abuse, neglect and manipulations in the spotlight, not the fact that he or she is a narcissist. Again, facts are very important and as much as an emotionally loving and compassionate- insightful society and court system would be ideal, the emotional layers and undertone are overlooked. Do not explain narcissism in any way! The style of manipulating truth from the narcissist can be so effective that it is more significant than truth itself.

❑ There is great power in silence. Silence provides space for truth and hidden things to come to light. Regardless of what is being said against you, the most effective thing you could do for yourself is to simply be silent. All of your partner's darkness, shadow, lies and buried anger will come powerfully to the forefront. Quite simply, the narcissist cannot stay silent in the midst of truth. They get worked up into anger and self- rage as a result of their lies and manipulations being exposed. The calmer you are the more they will fall apart. This cannot be stressed enough.

Mourning, Grieving and Letting Go

It may sound cliche or a given, but allowing yourself to mourn and grieve properly is essential for your healing. It can be appealing to take the easy route, telling yourself that you don't need to heal and that you are well and fine; however being with a narcissist is a very testing and harmful experience. It is natural to want to repress, deny or take the quick route, but this never works in the long run. Wounds are real and denying them can be detrimental to your growth. Also, remember the amount of mental, emotional and psychological pain your ex has caused! Just each one of these can have profound effects on your health, psyche and overall well- being.

So, to keep this section short and sweet, just a healthy reminder to allow yourself to mourn and grieve in order to truly let go. The tips and techniques, guidance and wisdom will help you to do this.

Chapter 4: BREAKING FREE

Overcoming Loneliness
(After Narcissistic Abuse)

A lthough being with a narcissist is a truly horrific and often traumatic experience, breaking free can lead to initial loneliness. You are so used to being with that person, being involved in their stories, games, and sense of companionship even if it is a twisted and mentally- emotionally abusive companionship; that finally leaving and being free can leave you feeling empty. This is natural- we are all chalices waiting to be filled. We need connections, stories, relationships and various realities to keep us feeling alive and fulfilled. So when you break free from the narcissist you are essentially an empty vessel. *What new stories are you going to create?*

This is of course in itself a beautiful process and fundamentally part of your journey. To be alone is to be all one, content, free and soulfully happy in your on independence. Once we remove attachments and stories which are no longer good for us, we provide ourselves the space and time for new stories; new realities and frequencies of being. I once heard the saying that life is like music. Life can be equated with music. We do live in a *uni*verse after all!

So, loneliness can be overcome by filling yourself with new stories- ones in *harmony* with your best interests and best possible expression of you.

Connected to this is a self- recovery, healing and boundary plan. Boundaries are very important, but so is your personal re- discovery of self and self- healing. Below are 5 key and highly effective ways to overcome loneliness.

1. Passion Projects

Immerse yourself in a passion project. New hobbies, favorite pastimes or creating a vision board to align with your dreams and aspirations can all be marvellous gateways back to your true self. Following your greatest joy allows you to overcome loneliness and heal from the sufferings caused by your narcissistic partner. Passion and fire are the spark of life, they re- energize and revitalize your inner core further enabling you to stop feeling isolated or cut off from the world. This is an unfortunate consequence of being the victim of narcissistic abuse or mind manipulations- you may feel disconnected to others on a profound level. Refinding yourself through a passion project is essential for your well- being.

2. Re- Finding Yourself ("Know thyself!")

Have you ever heard of the saying *know thyself*? This is knowing yourself on every level; your intentions, goals, dreams, hidden motivations and your personality in its entirety. We usually become lost and allow in the illusions and judgements of others when we do not know ourselves. 'The self' is the holistic part of being, the persona, characteristics and beliefs which make us unique. It is our thoughts, feelings, subtle impressions, emotions, past experience and deeper inner workings, also having a soulful aspect or significance. Recovering from a narcissist and refinding yourself tie in closely to knowing yourself, or knowing thyself. Not only can taking steps to rediscover and know thyself help you overcome loneliness, it will also help increase your self- esteem, self- worth and personal confidence.

3. Meditation

As briefly delved into earlier meditation is one of the most profound ways to heal from a narcissist. Feeling lonely is due to the feelings of separation or disconnectedness, and these all stem from your mind and emotions. Meditating *reconnects* you to your true self, inner harmony, and a sense of peace and well- being. It also expands your mind and allows you to be an observer of any chaotic, destructive or afflictive thoughts, beliefs or emotions. During the many months or years of narcissistic abuse you will have been through some terrible manipulative treatment. You may have been gaslighted, made to feel small, weak or inferior, or generally insulted on repeat. Your feelings, opinions, and perspectives may have been overlooked and where your beautiful qualities and strengths should have been supported, encouraged and cherished; you instead received neglect and abuse. All in all, your partner knocked your confidence and self- esteem in many unseen ways.

These all have profound negative effects on your inner belief systems, psyche and unconscious workings. Thoughts and emotions, which shape and define you as a person, are strongly influenced by experience and memories; so any abuse you may have suffered can become deeply ingrained. Meditation fills you with a "conscious emptiness," an empty space for new levels of thought, feeling and awareness. You may be able to access your higher self and higher mind, feel better and more positive about your life, and see all negative happenings as an opportunity for growth and new wisdom. In short, feeling lonely is replaced with feeling empowered.

4. Self- Therapy

The importance and power of self- therapy really cannot be undermined or overlooked. Self- therapy- any type of therapy that can be performed at home or in our own time- is great for mind, body, emotions and spirit. It is not just your thoughts and emotions which suffer during narcissistic abuse but also your soul, the core and hidden part of yourself. This is the part that allows us to feel love, empathy, a deeper connection to others and life's beauty; connect with music and access transcendental states, and develop advanced cognitive, intuitive and emotional frequency functioning.

Self- therapy incorporates a wide range of choices and channels so fortunately there is bound to be at least one route which works for you. Meditation, sound therapy, nature therapy, music, art, creative expression, spiritual literature, yoga, tai chi, massage, energy work and mindfulness are all forms of self- therapy. In fact, many people can change their whole mindset through the self- love and care which comes with engaging in therapy. Choosing to give yourself a healing massage, listening to soothing and peaceful music, and going for a mindful walk in nature or reading some soulful poetry can all be effective self - therapies in their own rights.

5. New Social Groups and Organizations

Balanced with all the other key ways to overcome loneliness and heal for the long term is the engagement of new social groups and organizations. This can include peer support, groups for victims of narcissistic abuse, or simply any organization or venture which allows you to feel good. Being happy and connecting with others is the best way to let go and move forward with your life, despite the initial loneliness you may feel. You can feel lonely or isolated in a group too as the truth is- loneliness is just a mindset. Some people feel lonely even when surrounded by family and peers, just as many feel most at peace and blissful when alone. True happiness and contentment comes from your ability to connect and feel at ease with the world. Taking the first steps by putting yourself out there will re-spark your passion for life and connection, and your connection with yourself.

Boundaries: Your New Power Word

Boundaries are your new power word! Breaking free and liberating yourself cannot occur until you put healthy boundaries in place. Not only do they need to be healthy but they need to be strong, so there is no chance of magnetizing or attracting another narcissistic relationship into your orbit.

Let's look at all the ways to create, develop and maintain a boundary plan.

1. Positive Self- Talk and Power Words

Positive self- talk may not initially appear as a form of boundary creating, however it is. Self- talk is the conversations we have with ourselves. When we engage in positive self- talk we open new neural pathways and actively influence the neurons in our brains. These neurons are responsible for the way we think, feel and respond to people, situations and experiences. They are also responsible for our communication, both internal with ourselves and external through our interactions with others. Just through positive and mindful self- talk, a natural boundary is created due to the ripple effect thoughts have on inner and external reality. In short, an invisible energy field is created through the power of the mind, thoughts and subtle intentions exhibited. This invisible energy field is your boundaries.

Connected to this is the effect of power words, specific words used with self- talk to enhance and amplify the power of your boundaries. Words can in fact be used- spoken or thought like a *mantra* or *affirmation* for optimum effect. Neuroscientists have discovered the incredible influence thoughts have on our physical being, emotions and over- all well- being or vibratory state (inner frequency), and this is backed up by a number of other schools of thought. Neuro- linguistic programming, cognitive behavioral therapy, and many alternative therapies and healing modalities all recognize and support the truth that our thoughts are powerful shapers and creators of our world. It is not only inner currents which are affected but worldly reality as we know it. So, harnessing the power of your mind in your boundary goals will allow your personal boundaries to expand and grow stronger, assisting you for the better.

2. Self- Affirmations

Connected to this are self- affirmations, or affirmations. Self- affirmations are essentially affirmations which can be spoken or thought during meditation or any contemplative activity for great effect. They are best performed as a sort of ritual or daily integrated habit. Taking time to dedicate some minutes to affirmations daily will enable your aura, your electromagnetic energy field to be strengthened and expanded and your mind strengthened. As the body is a complex and interconnected system, this has a profound effect on your emotions and thus increases your sense of boundaries on many levels. Mental boundaries, emotional boundaries, physical boundaries and spiritual boundaries are real, and once you begin to truly develop your own boundaries you will realize how 'one and the same' these all are. Once you strengthen one of your boundary muscles you can protect yourself from harmful or destructive energy. This includes the intentions and attempted projections of your narcissistic ex!

To engage in self- affirmations in an effective way, make time for a daily morning and/ or evening routine. This routine creates a structure in your life and an almost 'ceremonial' aspect. This is precisely what affirmations are, a sort of ceremony like meditation. Setting your intentions and committing to self- affirmations as a daily routine inevitably sharpens and strengthens your mind, further opening you up to new ways of perceiving. Included in this is protecting yourself and the connection this morning or evening routine has to self- healing and your aura.

3. Self- Healing/ Aura Strengthening

Kirlian photography has shown how there is an electromagnetic energy field surrounding each one us known as an aura to some. Spiritual beings, healers and energy workers have been aware of this energy field or aura for quite some time, however it is only in recent years where the science to support it has made itself known. All living entities have an electromagnetic energy field, from plants to animals and homo sapiens. This energy field is responsible for all thoughts, feelings, subtle impressions, beliefs, interactions, emotions, past memories and experiences, and one's general energy and vibration. We give off vibrations in every moment, and this is where the modern age term "vibes" has originated from. In terms of kirlian photography, one's aura can be seen to show just how real subtle energy and influences are. Science recognizes this 'invisible circle' responsible for our sense of boundaries as an electromagnetic energy field, whereas spiritual people and communities call it an aura. The term used is a technicality and regardless of your personal beliefs, what matters is the powerful and positive effects strengthening your aura has on your ability to protect yourself from the harm of narcissists. (Both the one currently leaving your life and all future ones.)

How do you strengthen your aura, you may be wondering? Self- healing is the key and fortunately there are many ways to do this. Meditation, engaging in therapy- either self- therapy or through seeking the help of others, and any sort of spiritual or healing activities and practices can all help you develop strong boundaries through aura-strengthening. There is so much guidance available nowadays through both Youtube and the internet and in presence, through teachers, workshops and practitioners experienced and qualified in their fields. Doing your own research at which route, if any, may be best for you may just be the secret missing ingredient to your perfected boundary plan. Many people are awakening to the spirit which flows through all living things and to our own spiritual power, and recognizing that the scientific electromagnetic energy field is in fact a powerful and very real aura! A boundary plan would not be complete without this aspect.

4. Physical Movement and Exercise: Strength

Strength is a key factor in your ability to be centered and aligned within. This alignment is to your own truth, self-respect and personal empowerment, which all come with strong and healthy boundaries. Physical movement and exercise strengthen you physically and with a strong body comes a strong character. The mind, body and spirit are designed to work in harmony, so improving your physical fitness and stamina has a positive effect on your character, willpower and mental- emotional boundaries. When you feel strong and centered through physical exercise you also feel more assertive, positive and deserving- deserving all life has to offer. This means you will *not* accept the ill- treatment or manipulations of a narcissistic ex you have fought so hard to separate from. Physical vitality, fitness and health inevitably makes you stronger, and this means you can put up better boundaries.

5. Emotional Muscles

Strengthening and developing your emotional muscles must be part of your boundary plan. Your emotional resilience, intelligence and connection are your keys to success. Empathy, intuition and an advanced to mature emotional connection to both yourself and others (the world around) allows you to stay centered within and aligned to your truth, own reality and choice to stay clear from narcissistic abuse, and the games of your ex. Emotions can be seen as a muscle, even if figuratively as they control and shape all of physical reality as we know it. We are essentially emotional creatures and those who are in tune with their inner empath (advanced empathy) or higher frequency functioning emotions can, literally, influence others and reality in a powerful and positive way.

Let's briefly look at the qualities associated with and necessary for a boundary plan with regard to developing and strengthening your emotional muscles.

Emotional Resilience

Emotional resilience allows you to adapt and respond to stressful or chaotic situations with ease and poise or grace. Your emotional health is strong and you know yourself well enough to not react. Life's difficulties and challenges can be overcome easily if not effortlessly based on the way you can recover, adapt and change with the tides.

Emotional Intelligence

Emotional intelligence is the capacity to be aware of and in control of your emotions. You can easily express yourself and possess a certain wisdom and empathy to you which reflects in your interactions and communications. Interpersonal relationships can be handled judiciously, fairly and maturely and you often shine light on others and situations. Emotional intelligence is a key trait to possess when dealing with a narcissist, specifically during the break- up and letting go period.

Empathy

Empathy allows you to possess all of the other key characteristics as to be empathetic is to literally feel what it is like to be another, or be in another's shoes. This allows you to deal with difficulties or strenuous interactions (with your narcissistic ex) in a way that is compassionate, self- respecting and wise. Possessing empathy and seeking ways to develop it allows you to increase your own boundaries, making them stronger through your ability to connect with a higher frequency (compassion, patience, empathetic- related qualities, etc).

Intuition

Intuition is your guiding light and your inner compass. It is also known as your gut or gut feeling, and can tell you which path to take or not to take in moments of need. It is also responsible for your instincts, instinctual awareness, your emotional wisdom, and your ability to know and follow your truth. Intuition connects you to a higher wisdom and awareness and to your seat of personal power- those strongly connected to their intuition know what to say and when, how to act and respond in each moment, and generally everything that will keep them on course. What better way to enhance and expand your boundaries than to develop, and connect to, your intuition?

Emotional Independence

Emotional independence is a sure way to develop and maintain boundaries. Acquiring this sets you apart from the entanglement you once suffered at the hands of your narcissist other (partner). When you are emotionally independent you have greater if not a certain chance of being free from mind games, manipulations, narcissistic entrapments and the general dark motivations and intentions of your ex.

6. Connecting to Your Spiritual Source

Finally, connecting to your spiritual source should be part of any boundary plan. The extent of this will differ for everyone individually, as everyone will have their own limits and be on their own journey. Spiritual source can mean many things to many different people; to some it can be as intense as spending days to weeks on a mountain meditating to a state of deep spiritual enlightenment. To others it may be recognizing spirit which runs through all of life and every living thing. The fundamental point is that connecting to spirituality or your own 'inner spirit', in any way, can have a profound effect on your personal strength. Boundaries come from strength and opening yourself up spiritually can make you mentally, emotionally or physically stronger too.

Some examples of connecting to your spiritual source for boundary improvement may include reading spiritual literature or poetry, meditating, engaging in transcendental meditation, going on a spiritual retreat, partaking in an ashram, learning about esoteric or ancient wisdom- or astrology, and connecting to your own inner nature and spirit through contemplative and introspective activities.

Dating After Leaving
the Narcissist

So how can you re- enter the dating scene after you have let go and healed from a narcissistic relationship? The best way to do this is to first identify the characteristics of narcissism and look to their opposite. Everything you don't want, seek to embody and integrate their polar opposite.

For example, narcissists are focused on physical beauty and appearance. Why not work on your *inner beauty*? We attract what we align with. Whatever you choose to focus on you inevitably draw into your orbit. It all starts with making the conscious decision and creating your world within. This way, external reality will shift and change to match it. The same is true for the tendency for narcissists to care primarily on materialistic success and physical identity, even when its not representative of their true personality or who they are inside. So in this respect, begin to re- align with true success and personal achievements in harmony with heartfelt or life- long-soulful dreams and aspirations.

Let's look at these in greater detail.

Attracting a New Partner Based on What You Don't Want:
The Opposite(s) of Narcissism

Inner Beauty

Narcissists are self- centered, egocentric and self- admiring. They're the type of people who stand in a mirror and only see their physical beauty, overlooking all of their horrible traits. You have just come out of a relationship where _your_ beautiful qualities were dismissed and even insulted entirely. Like Narcissus from the Greek mythological story, your ex may have been mistreating you psychologically and emotionally for a very long time. This plays on your conscious mind and your subconscious. So redefining your standards and what you choose to see as important in life can help you better attract a partner in harmony with your own values, beliefs and wishes. Inner beauty is a state of mind, heart, emotional maturity, and soul; it is who we are on the inside which ultimately reflects outwards into all of our interactions, relationships and bonds. See the inner beauty in both yourself and others and you will attract a mate on the same wavelength.

Real Success

Real success is birthed from service. How is someone bettering another's life? This is the question you should be asking and keeping in mind when dating again. Being mindful of the red flags, and perhaps re- learning them, helps with your ability to observe and steer clear of arrogance, egocentricity, self- righteousness and many of the other negative traits of a narcissistic personality. Like with soulful or heartfelt ambitions, dreams and aspirations described below, true success is born from pure and helpful intentions and a feeling of *connection* to others and the world at large. (As opposed who narcissists who are deeply disconnected to everything real, pure and selfless.)

Soulful or Heartfelt Ambitions, Dreams & Aspirations

Aligning with your own ambitions, dreams and aspirations in an authentic and real way will help you attract a partner on your wave. Narcissists are insincere, materialistic and egocentric with a false sense of superiority and success. They trick and manipulate people into thinking they are the bees knees, and further thrive off others adoration or love for them. Real ambition, dreams and aspirations help others in some way and almost always have some rooting in soulful, mindful or heartfelt service and intents. Perhaps you have lost touch with your own dreams and long term goals, or need to readjust and adapt to a more encompassing or focused vision? Recommitting to your personal goals and dreams can be a great catalyst into the dating world and finally finding your soul companion or the partner of your dreams.

Sincerity

Linked to the last point is sincerity. You want a partner who is sincere and authentic as these are two qualities your previous narcissistic partner was not. Manipulations, deception, mind games and facades of all sorts should not be welcome, so working towards sincerity in both yourself and a potential mate should be on the agenda. Sometimes we attract what we are, amplifying our own traits through others. Other times we attract our opposites into our lives to show us what we don't want. Either way, developing your own sincerity and being clear in your personal boundaries, wants and needs will allow you to date the right people, steering clear from narcissistic characters.

Kindness

Kindness is another personality and character trait you should look for. You may have initially been attracted to your previous partner's charm, bad boy or girl persona, or cold and "sexy" traits (as part of the narcissist seduction charm), however now you know what this can lead to you could better benefit from seeking kindness. Taking, selfishness and a lack of empathy and compassion define a narcissist, so turn towards their opposites. You will be glad you did! Kind is the new sexy.

Giving and Generosity

Like with sincerity and kindness, giving and generosity are qualities which should be at the top of your list. You can find these in those who work in the healing, care or animal or charity welfare professions. You may choose to hang out in related organizations or join a hobby or pursuit which allows you to connect with those in these fields. In addition to projects and professions which help others, giving and generous partners can be found in places which focus on spiritual or personal development. Why don't you join a yoga or meditation class? You could also volunteer at a local charity or organization seeking to make the lives of others, or the planet as a whole, better. There are so many expressions of a genuinely giving and generous nature. All you have to do is put yourself out there and align with them.

A Sense of Selflessness

If you don't want a future partner who is selfish aim for selflessness. This does not have to be extreme selfless-ness, but a healthy and sincere selflessness. Being selfish is focusing solely and predominantly on the self, on your self; which brings egocentricity and a lack of care, empa-thy and awareness for others. Selflessness is virtually the opposite, a concern and sensitivity for the needs and wishes of others above your own (something narcissists lack). Cultivating your own selfless nature and taking steps to attract a more selfless partner is one profound and powerful way to make sure you draw the right person to you. Again, seek places, organizations and institutions which help others connect to their own selfless nature. Perhaps your life partner is your own power couple?

Self- Awareness

Self- awareness is the most effective thing to develop and integrate to overcome the ignorance and arrogance of narcissism. With awareness comes greater insight, perception and intuitive wisdom; we learn how things should be and the best ways to interact and communicate based on past experience and how things shouldn't be. You don't want a partner who lacks all empathy, sensitivity and awareness for others, so readjust to a reality and subsequent partnership rooted in higher awareness. Higher awareness implies compassion, intimacy, morality and philosophy; conversation and connection firmly based in a kind, perceptive and dignified reality. Aim for self-awareness and attune your conscious mind accordingly. This will help you better attract a partner more in alignment with your own values.

Emotional Availability

Emotional availability and empathy are things you should now seek in a partner. You have already learned what you don't want and what doesn't work, and you can't get any further from emotional availability and empathy than a narcissist! Now is the time to redefine and commit completely to what you need in an intimate companionship. Just because you had bad luck the first time does not mean all dating partner's will be so narcissistic. You are wiser, more intuitive and aware, and stronger than ever before. Emotional connection is yours for the taking, giving and receiving. First make yourself emotionally available and then magnetize this into your orbit. Do not let in the fears or self- created doubts of what has been playing in your mind. You have already reached the light and are no longer in that tunnel!

Empathy and Compassion

Remember that the law of attraction is real. So whatever characteristics and personal attributes you seek to integrate, align with and embody- greater the chance you will find these in a partner. The universe is always conspiring *in* your favor, not against it. Now you have healed and freed yourself from a narcissist, you are better able to reconnect with those on your level. Developing your own empathy and compassion will greatly aid in this.

>>6

No Contact and Healing

At this stage the answer to this may be obvious. Narcissists as you are aware thrive off the acceptance and compliance of those who can be enticed into their mind games and manipulations. Any form of contact is a form of compliance in the narcissist's eye, as you literally feed them. They need others to keep their illusions and self- imposed identity in tact. Without you, the narcissist cannot keep fooling others (unless they start again and move, or find a completely new group of people to manipulate). In this sense, remaining in contact in the hope that they will have changed, you can still be friends, or simply that they now respect you for choosing self- love and leaving something which was not healthy for you, are all an illusion. Your partner does not respect you and is still a narcissist.

Separation in every physical sense including no contact or communication, unless it is a necessity regarding important physical matters (*children, finances and shared assets*), is essential for your healing and release. Any form of communication which keeps you in a bond is literally this- a bond; a karmic tie where you will always inevitably the victim, abused and sufferer. The only way you can break all ties therefore is to truly stay clear and go your own way. Any form of 'giving an inch' means that they will seek to take a mile, and just because you may have separated physically the narcissist's stories will still be in play. In their minds, they will always have one over on you or be in a position of control. A slight or single gesture of kindness, compassion, patience or tolerance on your behalf will be, unfortunately, seen as weakness and your ex will seek to use this against you. Even a tiny or nearly completely eradicated mental, emotional, psychological or physical manipulation which once had you trapped may resurface. Once again, you could find yourself under the narcissist's charm.

The best and possibly the only way to make sure this doesn't happen is to distance yourself, or at least make sure they are distanced from you. The duality and apparent opposing truth as to what has previously been shared is that the narcissist doesn't want you once you have actually cut ties and made it clear you can no longer be manipulated. Of course, they will always want you on a level, but they also are intelligent and aware to the fact that they can't get their fix if you are no longer appeasing them. As much as it may make them extremely annoyed, angry or frustrated (extremely being the key word here) even those with severe narcissistic personality disorder, who thrive on the compliance and unconscious support of others, know when to admit defeat. Your self- respect and decision to fully stop playing their games, appeasing and self- sacrificing way too much of yourself results in the "forced acceptance" that you are not someone to be abused. This means they need to find someone else, or work on themselves which may never happen.

Recovery, Integration and Moving Forward

Hopefully the chapters and information in this book has provided you with a complete and integrated understanding of your narcissist and how to move on, let go and heal. Re- finding yourself is a huge part of this as is engaging in self- therapy, healing and developing your personal boundaries. Two other things which need to be emphasized are *self- love* and *self- care*. It is very well exploring the complexity of the narcissist personality and motivations in depth, yet if you do not know how to move forward and recover through practical and realistically implementable self- love and self- care measures, it is not a very integrated approach to divorcing a narcissist.

To end this book we are going to briefly explore a "Self- Love and Self- Care" plan you can integrate into your daily routine, or at least take inspiration from to create your own.

"Self- Love and Self- Care Recovery Plan" for Healing & Moving Forward

1. Have a Morning Routine

Having a morning routine is crucial to your recovery and moving on. It keeps you motivated, dedicated to your own self- love and healing, and fully committed to your future. Habits are instinctual, we engage in daily habits all the time. Yet, once we become conscious of our habits we can evolve and develop them into routines which can best serve us.

A morning routine can include the following:

- *Saying thank you to your bed.* Gratitude is one of the most powerful forces and sets you up for your day. When you say thank you with sincerity, you are actively attracting more of the things you are grateful for. You are also increasing your over- all vibration. Upon waking, show gratitude towards the bed which has provided you comfort, peace and security. This will amplify your ability to utilize the law of attraction.
- *Drinking lemon water or herbal tea.* Lemon water helps clear your body of toxins and herbal teas

can kick start your immune system. *"Your health is in your wealth,"* and how true this statement is! Your thoughts, emotions, physical health and spiritual or holistic well- being are all intrinsically connected, so starting your day with something healthy, revitalizing, energizing and detoxifying-cleansing has a positive impact on your mind, emotions and sense of self- esteem and self- confidence. Confidence is connected to how you feel on a physical level, therefore incorporating something like lemon water or a detoxifying green tea into your morning routine will allow you to shine within. This reflects outwards!

- *Morning meditation.* Meditating upon waking or not long after can do great things for your self-confidence, self- esteem and ability to stay connected to your truth, further living your best life. Meditating increase energy vitality, sharpens your mind, enhances intuition, increases powers of observation and awareness, allows for higher thinking, and opens your mind to new ways of thinking, being and perceiving. It also helps enhance qualities such as empathy, compassion, kindness, sincerity and seeing the truth or wisdom in situations. It can help you be calmer and feel both happy and content inside, also stimulating advanced levels of imagination and creative thought. Merging a morning meditation into your daily routine may also open you up to new passion projects or paths for growth, connection and meeting new people.

- *Inspiring documentary or podcast.* Listening to an inspiring (or motivational) podcast or watching a documentary for just 10 minutes during your morning awakening period will do profound things to your self- worth, and stimulate you into action. This activity can help remind you of your own greatness and may spark creative, artistic or intellectual interests and talents. It will also remind you of how wonderful life is and why you are lucky to be alive!

- *Spiritual or inspirational literature, reading or poetry.* The same is true for reading. Poetry, spiritual literature or poetry, or any book which engages you and stimulates your emotions and mental thought processes in a helpful way should all be merged into your routine; or whichever one or two resonate. Anything spiritual, inspirational or motivational connects you to your own source of personal power and empowers you. You may receive memories or have flashback of joyful past experiences. You may be reminded of a past version of yourself, things you said or did or how you once inspired others. Reading not long after waking can spark you in unique ways.

- *Exercise or do a martial art.* Gentle exercise in the morning is known to improve all areas of life. It can move trapped energy, release stored emotions, provide physical vitality and wellness, and improve your mood and outlook on life. Engaging in a light martial art such as Chi Kung (Qi Gong) or Tai Chi is also highly beneficial. These two martial arts are very gentle and help to improve your internal energy systems. They also stimulate your inner spirit and core strength simultaneously whilst empowering you to master your mind, emotions and health.

2. Follow all the guidance in these chapters!

Finally and to conclude this book, follow all the guidance, wisdom and self- help examples in these chapters. You can try self- massage, self- healing, nature or music therapy, mindfulness and various self- development routes.

Conclusion

Divorcing a Narcissist by *Dr. Theresa J. Covert* is a carefully and compassionately constructed account of the narcissistic personality, often referred to as *Narcissistic Personality Disorder*, and how to release yourself from it's bonds. Narcissism can be a severe character deficit resulting in such an innate and apparent lack of empathy, kindness, care and love that it can almost be seen as borderline sadism. Depending on which type of narcissist you are dealing with, your psyche may have undergone a long and testing period of suffering, abuse and confusion, leaving you questioning your own abilities, self- worth and greatness. And this is what a narcissist fails to see- *inner beauty;* the qualities which make one real and authentic and lead to intimacy, vulnerability, and sincere and genuine human connection. Hopefully the chapters in this book will provide a long term recovery strategy with lasting effect. There is no quick fix, you must be willing to do the work and begin the journey to healing and wholeness. However, once you have you can be sure that your 'narcissistic other' will be your other half no more, and you can once again start afresh setting the reset button.

Made in the USA
Monee, IL
27 June 2024